JUST DON'T MAKE A SCENE, MUM!

ROSIE RUSHTON

Hyperion Paperbacks for Children
New York

First published in England by Piccadilly Press in 1995
Cover art by Giulia Orecchia

For information address Hyperion Books for Children, 114 Fifth Avenue, New York, New York 10011-5690.
First American Edition 1999
1 3 5 7 9 10 8 6 4 2

Printed in the United States of America.
ISBN: 0-7868-1370-9
Library of Congress Catalog Card Number: 98-89809

CONTENTS

1 The Phone-In

"*And that was East Seventeen with 'Stay Another Day'.*" Dean Laurie faded the record and grabbed a quick slurp of lukewarm coffee. "*And this is* On Your Marks, *the Saturday show that no kid with street cred can afford to miss.*" Ye gods, he sounded clichéd today. "*And now it's Moan Line time on the Hot FM—when you out there tell us up here just what's bugging you this week.*"

Cue jingle, "*Mo-oh-oh-oh Moan Line on 212 090Ny-aye-ine.*"

Another slurp of coffee. Remember not to swallow near the mike. Someone said that made you sound like a goldfish being flushed down the loo. "*And this week we're going to have our Moan about those oh-so-cringe-making times when you just want the pavement to open and swallow you up. Yes, we've all had them, haven't we? Times when we've opened our mouths and put our Doc Martens straight in!*"

Pause. Quick wave through the glass to the studio guest, Ginny Gee, local columnist and agony aunt on the *Leehampton Echo* who was engaged in making up her face as if she was about to front *The Big Breakfast*, not burble down a mike for fifteen minutes to the pubescent population of Leehampton.

"Or worse still, those occasions when your mum or dad make you look a real idiot in front of all your friends," Dean carried on. *"Or when big brother makes some cutting remark about the guy you fancy—just as he is coming into earshot? Couldn't you just die?"*

Dean paused to breathe in as Clarissa, the production assistant, ushered Ginny into the studio. Ginny squeezed her not insubstantial bulk past Dean, gave him a peck on the cheek, and plonked her bottom on the one vacant chair.

"We've got Ginny Gee from the Echo *here in the studio to help you sort out those blush-inducing, mouth-drying situations. And what's more, we'll be picking four of our callers for a great prize—more of that later. So pick up those phones and start dialling. You know the number—212 0909. And now it's two Unlimited with 'No one'."*

"Thanks for coming in, Ginny," he said. "Now all we have to do is sit here and hope that there are some embarrassed kids out there—there's nothing worse than a phone-in with no contributors."

"Oh, they'll ring in all right," said Ginny. "Most kids seem to spend their life in a state of terminal embarrassment."

She perused her burnt-orange fingernails critically and sighed. "And if my dear daughter is to be believed, parents are the prime cause. Do you know, Dean dear," she added, leaning toward him confidentially and enveloping him in a cloud of L'Air du Temps, "this morning my daughter told me I shouldn't go out in this outfit. Said fuchsia and orange didn't suit my skin tone. They're so conservative, today's kids, aren't they? I do look okay, don't I, Dean?"

Wise kid, your daughter, thought Dean. "You look teriffic, Ginny my sweet," he gushed. And then, thankfully, before he had to perjure himself any further, it was time to read the traffic news.

Outside the studio, the phones were starting to ring.

2 Behind Closed Doors

While Ginny Gee was applying the eighth layer of Hyper Rose lipstick and hitching up her Wonderbra in preparation for the fray, several members of her prospective audience were seriously considering leaving home.

In her bedroom in Wordsworth Close, with its Purple Ronnie poems on the walls and collection of pottery pigs on every available surface, Laura Turnbull was plucking her much-hated ginger eyebrows and debating whether you could have freckles surgically removed. She was supposed to be hunting for her lost history project, but then Laura rarely did what was expected of her. The entire world, she had decided, was conspiring against her. Not only was it her bad luck to have a father who had moved out to live with the Bestial Betsy and a mother who, instead of concentrating her efforts on dances or weddings and funerals, seemed to be dedicating her life to preventing her daughter from getting one.

If only Gran were here—*she* might sort Mum out. Jemma kept plucking up the courage to say something decisive but always chickened out. She hated rows and her mum was inclined to get really huffy if anyone argued. Whereas Gran was pretty cool for someone in their seventies. She lived in a state of perpetual chaos in a tiny mews cottage just off Brighton seafront with a tortoise named Maud and a mynah bird called Claw. Gran said life was for the living and told people to go for it and have a ball, grasp the nettle and give it a whirl. So why couldn't Mum, who was her only daughter, be like her? She resolved to write to Gran and ask her to come and stay.

This week Jemma had finally received an invitation to go somewhere really cool and her mother had said no because she didn't know the neighbourhood. Whose fault was that? Had Jemma wanted to move? Had Jemma wanted her father to get this stupid job in this poxy hospital in this grotty town? Her mum knew she found it hard making friends but her dad wanted this job—"the next rung

on the medical ladder," he called it—and that was that. But who was suffering for it? Jemma. And did her mother care? No way. She was too busy fussing over the twins and the pest Samuel and making sure that Jemma had a good hot breakfast inside her and clean socks on, to worry about her emotional and psychological traumas. If only her mother would read the back pages in her magazines she might realise that her daughter was at a critical stage in her development. But all Mum read were the recipes and instructions on how to make frilly pelmets and valances. And her father didn't care, because he was too busy cutting people open and yanking bits out to worry whether Jemma was being torn apart with emotional angst. Neither of her parents had a clue about her problems. Jemma wondered whether she qualified as a deprived child. She thought it was highly likely.

In the house next door to Jemma's, Jon Joseph was trying to use the music of East 17 on his new Walkman (which he'd bought with his fifteenth-birthday money) to blot out the strident tones of his father, who was dividing his time equally between packing his golf bag and holding forth

about his only son's shortcomings. All this had come about just because he wanted to go to The Stomping Ground tonight. His dad had started his nagging over the cornflakes and carried on non-stop through boiled eggs, toast and two cups of coffee. It was the usual stuff—what a pity it was he didn't put the same amount of effort into his studies as he did into his social life and how the world didn't owe him a living. Okay, Jon admitted his grades hadn't been too hot in the last lot of tests, but then, what was the point of continuing to slog his guts out to do something he didn't have his heart in? And no one else's parents expected their kids to study at weekends—although according to Dad, "You don't get to the top by finding excuses to stop working."

Dad was good at sounding off but not so good at listening. He had great ideas about Jon going to university and studying law and winning prizes. Only no one bothered to check what Jon wanted. He kept hearing about all the sacrifices they had made to send him to Bellborough Court instead of what his father called "the grotty comprehensive." He had never asked to go there. He hadn't asked for an hour's journey every day just so that his bluster-

ing father could boast at the golf club that his lad "went to private school." He wished his dad would let up a bit and realise that there was more to life than good grades. Well, he was going to the disco tonight, no matter what. And that was that.

Over on Wellington Road, Sumitha Banerji had banished her irritating little brother from the room and was standing in front of her bedroom mirror, scooping her long black hair up on top of her head to make herself look taller, and wondering whether phoning Moan Line would shame her parents into realising that they were stunting her development, turning her into a social outcast, and ruining her chances of ever getting to be presenter on *The Word*. Not only was she forbidden to cut her hair, varnish her nails, or wear makeup, but her father insisted on knowing exactly where she was going, with whom, and for how long. She hadn't even bothered mentioning the disco this time—she knew what the answer would be. The last time she had asked to go to The Stomping Ground, her dad had said, "That's not the sort of place that nice Bengali girls of your age go to," and her mother had looked apologetically at Sumitha and anxiously at

her husband but had not said a single word in Sumitha's defence. Her mother was a total wimp, Sumitha decided.

"If you had been brought up in Calcutta . . . " her father had continued.

"But I wasn't brought up in flaming Calcutta!" Sumitha had bellowed.

"I rest my case," her father had replied. "Your language shows what your English friends have done for your manners. The answer about the disco is, and will remain, no."

It just wasn't fair. They weren't in Calcutta. Sumitha only went there every three years for a holiday to see her grandparents. She was born in England, her friends were born in England. Why did her parents want it both ways? They came to England as students and stayed because they said the opportunities were so great. But they still insisted on bringing her and her brother up the same way they had been brought up in India when they were kids. Her father kept saying that young girls should have long hair as a sign of decorum. But *Shriek!* magazine said that short hair made you look taller. Sumitha had given up hoping that she would ever get beyond five foot nothing and if a haircut was

what it took to make her look sophisticated, then somehow she had to have one. Quite how she would face her father's inevitable wrath, she hadn't worked out yet.

A more pressing concern was tonight's disco. Her father said discos were undesirable and unnecessary. He was quite happy for her to go to drama classes and have tap and ballet lessons—good for her carriage and bearing, he said in that deliberate, staid way of his—but say disco to him and he went all tight-lipped and forbidding. Sumitha, for whom dancing was a way of life, couldn't understand the difference.

But this time she would beat them at their own game. Tonight they were going to a dinner dance at some posh hotel and staying overnight, and she was going to stay with Laura Turnbull. What her parents didn't know was that even now, Laura was persuading her mum to let them go to the disco. And even if Mrs. Turnbull phoned to ask if it was okay, Sumitha would be all right. Mum and Dad were leaving after lunch and her grandmother who was looking after her little brother, Sandeep, didn't speak good enough English to take phone calls. Sumitha reckoned she was home and dry. So there.

She turned the volume up on the radio and sang along to the charts. Her father hated pop music. Tough.

But it was over in Thorburn Crescent that feelings were running highest of all. Chelsea Gee was gazing into the Bugsy Malone mirror that her sister had brought her back from Chicago, desperately brushing her stubbornly crinkly, chestnut curls and willing a decidedly large and determined zit on her chin to disappear. She rather hoped her mother would do the same, but knew that was an idle hope. Fading into the background was not her style at all. In fact, she could win Oscars in limelight-hogging. She was a journalist and had a feature page in the *Echo* called "Speakout." The trouble was, she did. All the time. About love, sex, fashion (she, who wore orange miniskirts over her forty-one-inch hips)—she just went on and on.

Right now, Chelsea was praying that none of her friends were listening to the radio. Because, to add insult to injury, it was Chelsea's mum who was about to make another exhibition of herself on Radio Leehampton and it was Chelsea's mum—supposedly so understanding of the needs of

teenagers—who had said she had to be in by 10:30 P.M. from The Stomping Ground. So much for the person Radio Leehampton called "The Listening Mum with the Ear of the Young"! (I reckon that's against the Trades Descriptions Act, thought Chelsea.) Anyone with half a brain knew that leaving The Stomping Ground before 11:30 was certain social death. The radio station might well say that Ginny Gee's listening figures were huge but her daughter was not impressed.

SO YOU REMEMBER

Saturday 9.30 a.m.

Dear Barry,

Can you defrost mince and rustle up a bolognese or something? Nothing elaborate please, or the kids won't eat it. Gone to Radio L for the phone-in—why do I do it?

By the way, it's your turn to do the fetching-kids run tonight. I've told Chelsea she's got a 10:30 curfew. She's upstairs in a right old huff apparently, we're preventing her from getting a life. Funny—I thought it was the other way round.

See you later, Gin

P.S. Can you remind Warwick to have his cholera jabs?

P.P.S. There's a good job advertised in the <u>Guardian</u>—I've left it open at the right page. Why don't you apply for it today?

3

Chelsea Converses with Aardvark

Anyone observing Chelsea Gee that morning as she sat scowling at her reflection in the mirror would have been hard-pressed to discover what on earth could be causing such consternation. She had looks to kill for—thick, curly hair, amber-coloured eyes, and teeth so white and even that her dentist said she was putting him out of business.

Her bedroom was rather swish, too—what you could see of it under the mountain of magazines, discarded clothes, fluffy toys, compact discs, and empty Coke cans. Above her pine bed hung some Tibetan wind chimes and on the walls, in between the posters of Ryan Giggs and charts cut out of *Shriek!* magazine telling you how to get a supermodel figure in seventeen days, were Peruvian wall hangings, Balinese masks, and posters from French vineyards. These were all presents from Chelsea's sister, Geneva, who spent all her vacations from university backpacking or grape-picking or teaching foreign students how not to speak English.

On this particular morning, however, Chelsea was certain that nothing in her life would ever be right again. And as was her custom on such occasions, she was having an in-depth conversation with Aardvark, her battered but exceptionally long-suffering teddy bear. She hadn't named him Aardvark—that had been her linguistically inclined mother. "It was the first thing we ever bought you when you were a baby," she had been told a thousand times, "and aardvark is the first word in the dictionary." Other kids had bears named Ted or Pooh or Paddington, thought Chelsea. But then what could you expect from a mother who named her children after the towns where they were conceived? Geneva, Warwick, Chelsea. Thank heaven they gave up breeding before we moved to Leehampton, thought Chelsea. Just imagine—Lee Gee.

Chelsea squirted some Pretty Girl volumising spray on to her hair and turned up the volume on her radio. "Mo-oh-oh-oh Moan Line on 212 090Ny-aye-ine."

"Oh shut up! You want a moan—I'll give you Moan. It's her—my mother—your so-called agony aunt. Agony being the operative word."

This wretched programme was the last straw—Chelsea had never been so embarrassed in her entire life.

"I bet no other fourteen-year-old has to put up with this public humiliation on a weekly basis. And from their own mother at that. It's bad enough her being in the paper every five minutes, exhibiting her crinkled kneecaps to the entire universe—but at least my friends only read the stars."

Chelsea was referring to an article in the previous week's *Echo*, for which her mother was the ebullient features editor. It was called "How Old is Too Old for the Mini?" and carried a large picture, under which ran the caption, "Ginny Gee, mother of three, proves that even the over-forties look great in less!"

"I don't look bad for forty-five, do I?" Chelsea's mum had purred.

"You look very good, dear," Chelsea's dad had murmured, raising his eyes only briefly from *Gourmet Monthly*. (Years of experience had given him an innate awareness of when flattery was called for.)

"Puke, double puke," Chelsea had muttered.

"Pardon?" her mother had asked.

"Pretty," she had said meekly.

Indeed, so mortified had Chelsea been by this event that she had been moved to pen a poem on the agonies of exhibitionist parents.

ODE TO MOTHERS

Mothers are meant to be rounded
Gentle and soft and kind
Mothers are meant to wear sensible things
Blouses and skirts that are lined
Mothers should never be trendy
It simply just isn't right
When skin starts going all saggy
A miniskirt just looks A SIGHT!

She had left this masterpiece in a prominent position to the left of the Chardonnay bottle in the fridge, guessing—correctly—that her mother would head straight for a glass of wine after a hard day scribbling. To date, there had been little reaction. Chelsea felt let down.

"*We've got Ginny Gee from the* Echo *here in the studio to help you sort out those blush-inducing, mouth-drying situations*," chirruped Dean from the confines

confines of Chelsea's stacking system.

Oh great, thought Chelsea. She is a blush-inducing situation. If she cared about my feelings, she'd retire and do Meals-on-Wheels or write books for kids instead of making an exhibition of herself in full view of all my friends. But she just doesn't care.

"I bet Laura's mum will let her stay till midnight—but then Laura has a well-balanced and reasonable human being for a mother," she informed Aardvark. "Perhaps I could get Mrs. Turnbull to work on Mum—after all, they are bosom friends."

This idea rather appealed and Chelsea was about to phone her best friend with instructions for priming her mother, when her father called her.

"Chelsea, will you come down here and help with lunch?"

Oh, no—that's all I need—Dad and his culinary masterpieces, she thought.

Mr. Gee was one of those individuals who thoroughly enjoyed being a New Man. Since Frensham's Freshfoods had seen fit to dispense with his services as Marketing Manager (Creams and Custards), he was frequently to be found in the kitchen, wrapped in a shiny plastic apron with pots

of mustard all over it, creating an exotic dish for supper, or huddled in the cupboard under the stairs where he was busy growing shiitake mushrooms in an old bucket. He had quite a flair for food, he had discovered, although mundane things like egg and chips and beef stew held no appeal for his creative instincts.

Chelsea sighed. She adored her father; it was just that she didn't understand him. Her mum went around dressed in what Chelsea deemed to be totally unsuitable clothes, but at least she thought about what she wore. Her father, on the other hand, saw clothes purely as a method of keeping warm and the older and more dilapidated they were, the more he liked them. His current favourite was a sweatshirt with the logo of an inebriated penguin and a pair of suede shoes dating from the seventies.

"Chelsea, come on—I need a hand with the cooking."

Chelsea sighed to herself. "Why do I have to get involved in his gourmet creations. Why can't he just grill a fish finger?"

"CHELSEA! Now! I need your help!"

"Coming." Course, I blame Mum. If she was here being a proper mother I would be able to have a

normal childhood. Warwick's probably as dippy as he is because of maternal neglect.

Warwick was her nineteen-year-old brother, who had a chinful of acne and a desire to be a tree surgeon. Warwick went through life in a sort of comatose daze which worried Chelsea because, in a few weeks, he was setting off to backpack across Indonesia to look at bamboo forests and banyan trees. "It is doubtful," Chelsea had told her friends, "whether he will make it to Heathrow."

Chelsea had asked Warwick what he thought of their exhibitionist parent taking to the airwaves.

"They need the cash," he said, peering at what appeared to be a dying twig but which he assured would one day be a flowering cherry. "Hold these secateurs, Chelsea." So much for brotherly guidance.

"Chelsea! I am not going to ask you again."

"Coming!" She clomped downstairs, still muttering about the unfairness of life.

"At it again, Chelsea? First sign of madness, that, you know—talking to yourself!" said her father.

"It's the only way to get any intelligent conversation round here," retorted Chelsea. "What've I got to do?"

Her father immediately became businesslike and seized a wooden spoon with fervour.

"Right, we're going to make Pastel de Choclo and we need to work fast."

I like the "we," thought Chelsea. Still, chocolate couldn't be all bad.

Her father removed a solidified lump of minced beef from the freezer and examined it with the intensity of a surgeon about to perform micro-surgery.

"Where's the chocolate, then?" said Chelsea

"It's not chocolate, silly—it's a dish from Chile with meat and corn and eggs and black olives and loads of raisins . . . "

"YUK! That sounds mega repulsive!" said Chelsea.

Her father smiled benignly at her. "It's time you were more adventurous, Chelsea—there's a whole world of flavours out there and all you want is fried chicken and chocolate brownies. You will never educate your palate if you don't sample a few new dishes."

Chelsea thought it best not to comment.

"Dad . . . ?"

"Yes?"

"What do you think of this radio thing that Mum's doing? I mean, it's a bit much, isn't it?"

"Mmm—what?" Her dad was peering into the larder and hurling pots of spice over the counter top.

"The radio thing, Dad—can't you stop her doing it?"

"What on earth for? She loves it. And anyway, she's really good at that sort of thing. Sorting other people out has always been her forte. She's a getting-involved sort of person." He peered into the depths of the larder. "Someone has eaten nearly all the raisins—that's all I need." He glared accusingly at Chelsea.

"Don't look at me—I expect Warwick's had them," said Chelsea.

"Bother it—they're an essential ingredient," said her father.

"Don't worry, we can have spaggy bol," said Chelsea with relief.

"No, no, this calls for a little initiative," said her father with glee. "I wonder whether prunes would work as well?"

Chelsea's stomach threatened violent action. She decided not to think about it.

"But Dad, I mean—when Mum does all these stupid stunts for the paper, or spouts on the radio about teenage sex and stuff, don't you just want to die?"

"No, why on earth should I? It's not me that has to do it. Or take the advice." He chuckled at his own wit.

"Actually, I'm rather proud of her," he continued, chopping onions. "And besides, she enjoys it—in a way, she's trying to find herself, I think."

Just then, Warwick ambled into the kitchen. His tall, scrawny body seemed to be at ill at ease with its surrounding and his face wore an expression of permanent bewilderment.

"I'm off to the garden centre," he muttered, peering at Chelsea through his glasses. "Is that a spot on your face, Chelsea?"

"Oh go pot a seedling!" snapped Chelsea.

Warwick picked up a handful of sliced onion and an olive.

"Your mother said to remind you to get your cholera jab," said his father. "We don't want you going down with something nasty in the intestines."

Warwick turned pale, replaced the olive, and wandered off.

"Switch the stereo on in the sitting room so I can hear your mother, will you?" Her dad patiently took another onion from the basket and chopped away methodically. He arranged the meat and eggs and olives in a dish and looked at it in an admiring sort of way.

Chelsea fled upstairs and flung herself down on the floor. "I'm switching it off once this record is over, whether you like it or not," Chelsea told Aardvark sternly. "I can't bear to listen to her—she's bound to go all virtuous and sanctimonious and give little pieces of motherly advice about tampons and boyfriends—and all my friends are sure to be listening. And she is so out of date, you'd just die to hear some of the things she trots out. Or else she tries to sound so cool and with it—and makes it quite clear to the world at large that she is totally without it."

"*And now it's time to talk to Ginny Gee…*"

"Oh no, here we go. She's on. I'll turn it off." She flicked the controls. Silence reigned. Chelsea bit her fingernails. She turned it on. "I can't—I need to know the worst. I can't listen. I must listen. Please, please make her be normal. Just this once. Please."

Chelsea's intercession to the Almighty was interrupted by the shrilling of the telephone.

That better be for me, thought Chelsea. I need to have my mind taken off my tragic home life.

Laura Enlists Chelsea's Help

"Leehampton 554901—Chelsea. . . ."

"Hi, Chelsea? It's me, Laura."

Great, thought Chelsea. Now I can get tonight sorted. But Laura had other ideas.

"Listen, I've got to talk really fast because if Mum catches me on the phone she'll do a melt-down. She's into one of her if-you-devoted-the-time-to-your-schoolwork-that-you-devote-to-talking-you'd-still-be-top-of-the-class bits. I forgot that our history project has to be finished by Monday. Mum thinks I am in my room dealing with the causes and effects of the Peasants' Revolt."

"Oh no, it's not this Monday that it has to be done, is it? Can I have a peek at yours?" pleaded Chelsea. Laura was one of those people who could produce three pages in ten minutes, even on a subject she knew nothing about. She was what Mrs. Hopkirk called a high flyer.

"Yeah, if you like—much good it'll do you. I've done all of two sentences so far. I've got far more important things on my mind. You see, your mum's on..."

"I know, I know," sighed Chelsea, "she's on On Your Marks. Don't blame me. It's awful, it's gross, but I can't do a thing about it. You can switch the radio off—I have to live with her."

"You don't know when you're well off. At least your mum knows how to behave and . . . "

Chelsea spluttered. "Behave? Get real! My mum's never known how to behave."

"Well, just try living with mine," said Laura. "Your mum's really cool. I mean, she'll talk about anything, you only have to say 'boy' to mine and she turns puce and thinks I'm about to take part in an orgy. She should talk," she added ruefully.

"Mine would be so busy minding everyone else's business, she wouldn't even notice if I did," muttered Chelsea, degunging her left ear with one finger. "Anyway, what were you going to say?"

"Well, you know you're supposed to phone in with all these embarrassing situations and stuff?

They're giving away prizes as well—they haven't said what yet . . . "

"A day at the *Echo* with my sainted mother, I bet," interrupted Chelsea

"Oh, that would be brilliant," said Laura enthusiastically. "I could use it in my book."

Some people are easily pleased, thought Chelsea. But then Laura was a very literary sort of person who wrote for the school magazine without being asked to, and read all sorts of erudite books. Chelsea, on the other hand, preferred test tubes to Tolkein any day and would rather create a noxious gas than a clever essay.

"Anyway," continued Laura, "I was just wondering whether I could phone and get your mum to kinda sort my mum out—you know, with this awful business with the geek Melvyn. Before she makes a complete prat of herself."

"Oh, come on, Laura, you can't do that! My mum will recognise your voice, and whose side do you think she's going to be on? She gets on with your mum like a house on fire."

"That's it, you see," said Laura triumphantly. "If I phone in, using a different name but giving all the details, your mum will guess it's me. Once she realises the agonies my mother's behaviour is putting me through, she'll have a quiet word with her about not ruining my life. Your mum understands things like that. And because my mum thinks yours is the bee's knees, she'll take notice and do as she is told."

"I wouldn't be so sure," muttered Chelsea, whose experience had taught her that people over the age of twenty-five rarely took any notice of anyone.

Laura sighed. "Well, I have to do something, I can't stand it much longer—I mean slobbering outside the supermarket in full view of all my friends, that was the final straw. I nearly died. I mean, at their age. Anyway, can I come round to your house and phone in? There's no way I can do it from here. Mum is sure to hear."

Chelsea was not convinced that this was a good idea, but she knew Laura well enough by now to know that when she got hold of an idea, she wouldn't budge. It was easier just to go along with it.

"Well, okay then, but you'll have to be quick. Tell you what, I'll dial in, give a false name, and then you'll be in the queue. But hurry."

"Okay. Thanks." Laura sighed again. "I do wish I

had a normal mum like yours."

"The word normal is not compatible in the same sentence as any reference to my mother," said Chelsea. "See you in about five mins."

5 Jon Kicks at the Traces

Laura was not the only person that Saturday morning who was having parent trouble. Over on Billing Hill, where the houses had names like Chatsworth and Broadlands because their owners wanted to sound as if they lived in stately homes even though their bank balances only ran to mock Georgians with double garages and burglar alarms, Jon Joseph was having a row with his father. Again. Or rather, Mr. Joseph was holding forth at some length while Jon watched his podgy lips moving to a background of pop music blaring from his Walkman.

No one would have guessed that Jon and his dad were even distantly related. Mr. Joseph was red-faced, rather overweight, and inclined to like the sound of his own voice. Jon was lean, angular, and had hair that curled into the nape of his neck—a feature that caused a number of girls at his private school to swoon with delight. His long legs, permanently tanned from weekends spent out on his mountain bike, were another source of female approval.

"Oh, do take those wretched things out of your ears when I am speaking to you," his father, Henry, shouted, wrenching the cord from his ears. "I don't suppose you have heard one word that I have said to you," he blustered, his three chins wobbling as he rammed another golf club into his bag.

"It doesn't matter," retorted Jon, "I've heard it all before, a million times. How does it go now—'After all we've done for you, all the sacrifices we've made, the least you can do is put some effort into your studies.' Oh yes, and then there's the bit about 'God gave you a good brain—try using it,' and 'If only I'd had the opportunities you've been given.' Have I missed out anything?"

"You can be insufferably rude at times, Jon," said his father. "You know how much you want to get to Cambridge and . . . "

"Hang on a minute. I want to get to Cambridge? No way. Isn't it really a case of you and Mum making your minds up ages ago that nothing but Cambridge will do? That only that way will you have something else to brag about at the golf club and Rotary?"

His father glared at him. "Now look here, Jon..."

At this point Jon's mother padded into the kitchen with an armful of flowers. She was tiny, especially when viewed against the rotund bulk of her spouse. Dressed in a chiffon kaftan and embroidered slippers, she looked as if the merest puff of wind would blow her over. This was misleading. She was a lot tougher than she looked.

"Out of the way please, both of you—I've got to get three bridesmaids' posies done by eleven o'clock." She dumped the flowers on the worktop and reached for the scissors.

"I was just trying to get the lad to see sense, Anona," snapped her husband. "I've told him, with a brain like his, he should . . . "

Mrs. Joseph, who had heard it all a dozen times before, said nothing and rammed a couple of rosebuds into a wire frame.

"Dad, will you listen to me for once!" shouted Jon. "I don't have this amazing brain you keep going on about. It's all in your mind. Ever since I can remember it's been 'Jon's such a bright lad, he's going to Cambridge, aren't you, Johnnie?' Well, I'm not, and that's that."

Mr. Joseph, who took little pink pills for blood pressure and whose already florid complexion was turning more puce by the moment, grabbed his golf bag and strode to the back door.

"Well, just look at me, that's all I can say," he expostulated. "Had to work my way up the ladder by my bootlaces—no one gave me a head start. I got where I am today through sheer grit and determination. You've had it all handed to you on a silver plate and you just don't appreciate it." He growled and turned to his wife. "I'm off now—perhaps you can knock some sense into your son."

Mrs. Joseph noticed that Jon was always her son when he was not behaving as his father wished, and his when he scored a half century for the school eleven.

As the back door reverberated to his father's departure, she looked at her son and said, "Why do you wind your father up like that, Jon? You know how set he is on your making a success of your life."

Jon perched on a kitchen stool beside his mother. "But my idea of success and his are poles apart—

I don't want to spend the rest of my life stuck in some grotty office all day pushing papers round a desk," grumbled Jon.

His mother sighed. She didn't often air her views—her husband did enough of that—but she did see Jon's point. "It's just that he wants you to have all the things he would have liked but couldn't have," she said, not wanting to seem disloyal to her husband.

"But I'm not Dad. I don't want the things he wanted. I don't want to be the sort of person he is. I don't want to go to any university. And I don't want to be stuck in some school where I have to… "

His mother interrupted. "Hang on a minute. 'Stuck in some school'? Do you have any idea of what it costs us to send you to Bellborough Court? What sacrifices your father makes to find the fees? How I work at a boring old job to top up the funds? We are giving you the best possible start in life."

"It's my life, in case you haven't noticed," yelled Jon. "I am fifteen and a half—anyone would think I was doing A levels tomorrow. And I didn't ask you to pay school fees—I could have gone to Lee Hill with all my friends from primary school. But Dad wouldn't have it."

"Oh Jon, how could you compare Lee Hill with Bellborough Court? Don't be silly—most kids would give their eye teeth to go private." And most mothers would give their eye teeth not to have to work weekends to help pay for it, she thought silently and immediately was swamped with guilt for being so selfish.

Jon sighed. There was no point arguing. He had plenty of friends at Bellborough but none of them lived nearby. His best friend, Rob, was at Lee Hill and so were Gavin and Ben and Doug. They seemed to be doing great. And having fun at the same time. Not that his dad seemed to think fun mattered. Well, he would jolly well have some fun tonight.

"By the way," he said, "Rob's dad is picking me up at seven-thirty to go to the disco."

His mother sighed. "That'll be nice—but don't expect your father to approve."

"He's not invited," said Jon. "Anyway, my whole life does not revolve around work. I want some fun. Didn't you ever want fun when you were my age?"

His mother said nothing. There were a lot of things she had wanted when she was Jon's age, and she hadn't got any of them. Which is why it was so

important that Jon didn't miss a single opportunity. But nevertheless, she did want him to be happy. Lately he had seemed preoccupied, as if there was something he wanted to talk about but just didn't get around to. A bit like she had been when she'd first married Henry, she thought ruefully.

Jon took the silence as a promising sign. "Actually, Mum, I think I'm more like you than Dad. I mean, you're really good with colour and design and stuff. You see what I really want . . . "

"Yes, Jon? What do you want—or are you just drifting through life with no direction?" Like me, she thought. He mustn't end up like me.

Jon snatched his earphones up from the floor where they had fallen. "I'll tell you what I want. Right now, the only thing I want is to get the hell out of here and as far away from all this constant nagging as I can. I'm going out."

"Jon, where are you going? Jon, come back—I didn't mean—tell me what…"

But Jon had gone.

6
Laura Takes a Tumble

Laura said good-bye to Chelsea, hung up, and grabbed her jacket from the solitary hook in the tiny hallway, tripping over her mother's umbrella and kicking the telephone directory on her way. This poky little house was the pits. She was sure that her friends talked about it behind her back. Their old house had had big rooms and plenty of space to make a mess in—this one was no bigger than a dog kennel and half as attractive. It had no atmosphere, no charisma and simply wasn't the right environment for a creative genius. She didn't know how her mother could have chosen it—but then, these days her mother not only seemed totally oblivious to the sheer ignominy of moving to 18a Wordsworth Close, but completely unaware of a whole load of deadly embarrassing things that were happening in their lives. Mum had changed and Laura didn't like it. Not one bit. And what was more, she wasn't prepared to put up with it for very much longer.

Laura wasn't at all like her mother—Mum was blonde while Laura had auburn hair like her dad ("And a temper to match," her gran would mutter from time to time), and Laura's mum was slim while Laura was a bit on the chubby side. (This was due largely to the fact that she saw chocolate biscuits and cheese and onion crisps as life-sustaining items to be devoured at regular intervals.) What's more, Laura's mum was very dependable, cool, calm, and collected, which no one, not even Laura herself if she was being really honest, could say she was. Mum was great in a crisis but Laura flew off the handle at the slightest provocation. "Virginia Woolf did the same," she would tell her friends on occasions when they got tired of her tirades. They never seemed that impressed.

After Dad had moved out, Mum had said she would have to get a job. Laura didn't like that idea, even though then Mum wouldn't have any excuse to keep putting off buying Laura new clothes. It was just that she didn't want people to know her mum had to go out to work for money. Laura and her mum had got on really well—until Melvyn. Laura

blamed him for the change in Mum. These days Laura didn't know where she stood—one day Mum would be all airy-fairy and devil-may-care, the next she could snap everyone's head off and lay down the law about everything from apple cores under the bed to the time Laura spent on the phone—which was hardly any time at all really. And more often than not, Melvyn would be at their house for supper, or mowing the lawn, or helping her mum wallpaper the loo and grinning at Laura with that inane smirk of his, and trying to be all matey. It was too much.

Grandma said it would take time, that Laura should try to help her mother through this difficult patch in her life. She did try to be nice but there were times when she wanted to yell, "What about my life? Was it me that drove Dad away into the arms of the Bestial Betsy? Was it me that moved from the decent house in Preston Abbott where I had my own shower room and a huge garden to go and write my novel in, to this seedy little semi on this grotty housing estate with a lawn the size of a postage stamp? But it's me who is having my entire life ruined at a crucial time in my social and intellectual development. I'm the sort of kid Oprah

Winfrey talks about in muted tones of sympathy and understanding."

Yanking her bike out of the cramped little garage, and shouting to her mother that she was going over to Chelsea's, she pedalled as fast as she could out of the close and on to Church Farm Road. Chelsea lived three minutes away in fashionable Thorburn Crescent, where the houses stood back from the road and driveways were crammed with Mercedes and FourTraks. Chelsea's family were really rich—well, Chelsea said they weren't, but Laura reckoned they had to be because Chelsea's mum was a journalist and did stuff on the radio and wore clothes from boutiques instead of chain stores and was always smiling. Laura noticed that people with cash found being light-hearted a whole heap easier than people who were working out whether to pay the gas bill or eat. And even though Chelsea's dad was out of work right now, they still had takeaways most Saturday nights and got videos out without anyone complaining about the £2.50. Chelsea, sighed Laura, had it all. She even got A grades in physics and chemistry.

I bet Chelsea's mum never yells at her, thought Laura as she waited for the traffic lights to change.

Because she realises the damage that sort of thing can do to kids. And I'm pretty sure she would never take up with a boring old fart like Melvyn when she could have Dad.

That was another thing Laura envied Chelsea for—her dad was still living at home.

Everyone had been really surprised when Dad moved out. "He always seemed such a solid sort of chap," Laura's uncle had said. "How strange," Laura's aunt had murmured. "And him a chartered accountant," sniffed Mrs. Bramhill next door, as if an ability to understand profit and loss accounts was a certain recipe for everlasting marriage.

Dad had moved in with the Bestial Betsy—probably because he was trying to get over the pain of being rejected by Mum, Laura reckoned. He couldn't actually like Bestial B more than Mum—Betsy had black hair and a big nose and wore Laura Ashley skirts and sweaters with lace collars and picked things off bushes by the roadside and made them into wine and other strange concoctions. Laura thought that there was a pretty good chance she had latched on to Dad for his money (the money Mum said she never got to see) and was brewing elderflower wine to conceal the arsenic she was

planning to pop him off with. She told Grandma that she thought the Bestial Betsy was up to no good, and didn't she think they ought to go to the police, but all Grandma had said was that Laura was far too inclined to overdramatisation and she blamed Ruth Rendell and The Bill and Casualty in equal parts.

Laura reckoned her mum was being really horrible about her dad. They had had a bust-up about it only yesterday. Laura's grandma, who always came to supper on a Friday, said, "Did you get that cheque from Peter?" and Laura's mum had replied, "What do you think? When did that man ever part with ten pence when he didn't have to?" and Laura, who was feeling grotty because her period was due and she had got a C-minus in biology and she detested liver casserole, and because she loved her dad and hated him for not being there, had burst into tears and said, "You're always being rotten about Dad! That's why he left—no one would want to live with YOU! I hate you! I wish I wasn't living here in this dump either!" and she had pushed back her chair and stormed out of the room.

She had flung herself on to her bed, crying as noisily as possible so her mum would feel really guilty and come and say she was sorry and that she realised it was all her fault, and she would ask Dad to leave the Bestial Betsy and come back to live with them and everything would be fine. They would move back to their old house and life would be normal again. But after twenty minutes of sobbing and making choking noises and flinging herself off the bed on to the floor (which hurt more than she meant it to), she realised that her mum was not taking any notice.

That was the problem, she thought as she freewheeled down Billing Hill toward Chelsea's turning. Mum never took any notice of her feelings or opinions anymore. Come to think of it, Mum never took notice of anything, from peeling paint on the windowsill to the fact that Melvyn was a pasty-faced, humourless git. It was as if she didn't care. What was it that Mum used to say to her when she was little and having a tantrum? "Don't care was made to care." Well, Laura had decided it was time to take action.

She was so absorbed in her thoughts that she did not see the red mountain bike careering out of a driveway on the left. Well, not till its front wheel interlocked with hers, that is. There was an awful

squealing sound, a scrunch, and she found herself gazing up at a spinning bicycle wheel and a boy with wickedly curly hair and amazing legs who looked distinctly displeased with the whole incident.

"Are you mad or what?" he yelled, disentangling his Walkman lead from her handlebar and staggering to his feet. Laura just lay in the kerb and stared at him.

7
Jon Gets Diverted

This was all he needed. Thwarted ambitions, another blazing row with his father, and now some stupid kid crashes into his precious bike.

Jon scrambled to his feet and picked up the bike. There was a scratch on the wheel guard and the gravel had pitted the paint at the back, but at least nothing was dented or bent. But all his sketches for the cover of the school magazine which had been hidden in his saddle bag were all over the road. Ruined, probably. Pestilential kid.

The girl was struggling to her feet and as he scrabbled around picking up sheets of grubby paper, he noticed that her hands were grazed and her left cheek was bleeding. She was also staring at him in a rather disconcerting manner.

"Don't you ever look where you are going?" he snapped, suddenly feeling ill at ease and awkward as he brushed mud off his drawings and tried to look nonchalant even though he had suddenly realised that his right elbow was stinging like crazy.

"Me? Me?" yelled the girl, green eyes blazing. "If you recall, I was minding my own business on the right side of the road. It was you that came down that drive like a bat out of hell and straight into my path. So don't you go putting the blame on me, dimbo!"

Jon stared at her. He'd expected her to burst into tears or say she was frightfully sorry about his bike. She had spunk, he'd give her that. Must be all that ginger hair that made her so fiery. Come to think of it, she had a really interesting face. Jon was fascinated by people's expressions, their gestures, the way they reacted. But right now, he hated the universe and everyone in it. And she was the last straw.

"I'm surprised you're allowed out on the road on your own—you shouldn't be in charge of a doll's pram, never mind a bicycle!" he shouted. "Brainless kid," he muttered for good measure.

"If it's brain we're discussing, you're the one lacking in grey matter," said Laura. "See these? These are called brakes. When you apply them a bicycle slows down." She separated each word deliberately as if talking to a dim-witted foreigner. "Most people

slow down when approaching a road. Most people look where they are going. People who are not bad-tempered egotistical idiots, that is." (She'd discovered the word *egotistical* last week and thought it had a nice ring to it. She was planning on using it in The Novel.) She gave a sarcastic leer, and turned away.

Suddenly he grinned. "Okay, okay—truce. I was in a right ruck when I came down the drive. I wasn't thinking straight, never mind riding properly. Parent trouble." He raised his eyes heavenwards.

"You and me both," murmured Laura.

Jon looked at her hands. "You sure you're all right?"

Oh heck, he was going to be nice to her. She could cope with ranting and raving but his smile had made her go all wobbly round the kneecap area.

"Yes, I'm fine," said Laura. "Sorry about the..."

"No, forget it. I'm Jon, by the way."

"I'm Laura. What are those?" Laura pointed to the pile of papers in Jon's hand.

"Oh, nothing—just stuff—homework stuff," he muttered.

He wished she wouldn't stare at him like that.

He suddenly felt clumsy and awkward and knew his face was going bright red. And he was sure she was staring at those awful whiteheads on his chin. "Well, I must dash—things to do, people to see." He stuffed the drawings back into his saddle bag and this time remembered to buckle it up.

Laura picked up her bike, still gazing at him and saying nothing.

"See you around," he said. And with that he jumped on his bike and sped off down the hill. Laura didn't move.

I think, she thought to herself through the throbbing pain in her cheek, I think I am in love.

8 The Phone-In Heats Up

Back at the radio station, things were moving apace.

"So we've had Russell, whose mum still expects him to wear handknitted sweaters, Trish whose older sister flirts with her boyfriend, and Melanie whose mother queue-jumps at the checkout by pretending to feel faint." Dean Lourie beamed at Ginny. *"And all of you will go into the Prize Draw to win a trip behind the scenes of the* Echo*, personally conducted by Ginny Gee."*

Big deal, thought Chelsea, as she dialled the number.

"So keep those calls coming in. We're going to take a break now for the local news and weather, but we'll be back and so, I hope, will you."

Dean leaned back in his chair and smirked at

Ginny. "Right, Ginny, what have we got lined up for you after the break?" He glanced at his computer screen, where all the waiting calls were logged.

"There's a Samantha from Little Brafield—brother keeps teasing her about being fat, Kirsten, age thirteen—embarrassed by her lisp, Sumitha—bit of bov with parents who . . . "

"Oh no, Dean—put that one to the end and then say we're out of time. My daughter goes to school with a girl called Sumitha and I know the family—if it turns out to be the same one—and there can't be many Sumithas in Leehampton—it could cause all sorts of difficulties," sighed Ginny.

"Okay. Then there's Mia whose dad was had up for speeding—by her boyfriend's dad who's a copper (what a laugh!), and then Becky age fourteen—probs because her dad and mum have split up. That all A1 okay with you?"

"Sounds fine to me," said Ginny, peering into her handbag mirror and patting her hair.

"News is just ending, Gin. Piece of muse, and then you're on. All right?"

"Sure, Dean. I'm all yours."

Thank goodness you're not, thought Dean as he brought the sound up on Take That.

Down the Line

"You took your time—what kept you?" Chelsea stood back to let Laura through the front door. "Hey, Laura—you're filthy! What happened?"

"Tell you later—did you phone Moan Line?"

"Yes, and what's more, I thought you were going to miss it. You have to give your phone number to this woman and then she phones you back. So I pretended to be you. Only she's already phoned back and we're hanging on. Quick."

"You didn't go and give my proper name, did you?"

"No, idiot—you are now Becky. I bet it doesn't work—I mean, my mum may be crazy but she isn't thick—she's bound to suss it's you."

"I keep telling you—that's the whole point," snapped Laura. "She's a really together person—she'll realise the damage being done to my life and sort my mum out and everything'll get back to like it was before."

"If you say so. Anyway take this," Chelsea threw the receiver at Laura. "You have to listen down the phone to what's on air till they announce your name."

"I'm nervous," said Laura.

"Think of Melvyn," advised Chelsea. Laura pulled a face and made vomiting noises.

"Becky—are you there?"

"Hey, it's me," Laura whispered, waving an arm in Chelsea's direction.

"Becky? Hi, this is Moan Line and I am just putting you through to Ginny."

"*Hello there, Becky—and what's your embarrassing dilemma this morning?*" Ginny's cheerful voice boomed down the line.

"*Um, well, it's my mum, actually. You see, she's split with my dad and she's got this new man and to be perfectly honest, he is gross. I mean, really gross. But she can't see that.*"

Laura took a deep breath.

"*The thing is, she is behaving in a really embarrassing way. I mean, they even kiss and cuddle in public. Outside shops and in pubs and things. I've told her she shouldn't carry on like that at her age—making a complete idiot of herself, and me, but she just laughs or else she yells at me and says I don't understand and that she's only having a bit of fun."*

"Well now, is that the root of the problem, Becky?" said Ginny, in what she hoped were understanding tones. *"Do you resent her having fun?"*

"Well, no, of course not—but I mean, she's being so embarrassing. She's got girlfriends—if she's lonely, she can go out to the cinema with them or play tennis and things like that." Laura gulped. *"But anyway, she should be trying to get my dad back, not wrapping herself all round this geek."*

"Geek." Ginny had heard that word before when Laura—oh no. Ginny cleared her throat and pulled a face at Dean. He wasn't looking. *"Well now, Lau—Becky,"* she began, *"you know, your mum is probably just getting over a very upsetting episode in her life. She needs friendship and affection—love, even. And of course, just because people show affection to one another, it doesn't mean they're about to run off into the dark blue yonder together."* She laughed in what she hoped was a reassuring manner.

Laura was just a little bit worried that she might cry. *"But she should be with my dad—not him!"*

Ginny was making wild gestures with her arms at the production assistant behind the glass. "Try to

get rid of her," she mouthed. The production assistant was too busy answering the telephone to notice.

"*Well, La . . . er, Becky, I think that perhaps your dad and your mum are having their differences right now, and only they can work out what is best for them. Your mum needs you to try to understand that. I mean, you must have some friends she doesn't like—just as she has one you don't much take to. Perhaps you could sit down and…*"

"…have a calm and reasoned discussion about your feelings and work out a way of handling them together," mouthed Chelsea at Laura.

"*…have a calm and reasoned discussion about your feelings and work out a way of handling them together,*" said Ginny. "*I hope that helps, dear.*"

She aimed a stiletto at Dean's kneecap and flapped her hands frantically. "*Ah, yes, well, thank you, Ginny Gee, and that is all we have time for today on Moan Line.*" Dean Laurie slid the control lever up the console and the sounds of Understated Style swamped the studio.

"Prob?" he enquired. Ginny wondered why disc jockeys always talked in abbreviations.

"Sort of—that was a friend of my daughter's trying to pretend not to be." She took a slurp of what the station laughingly called coffee. "Little madam—honestly, these kids, they think they have the answers to everything."

She sighed. "Dear me, poor old Ruth Turnbull—caught snogging outside the supermarket."

"Pardon?" said Dean, looking bewildered.

"Nothing," said Ginny. "I'm off home to face the music. See you next week."

"I'm not too sure that was much help," said Laura miserably. "I mean, I know she's your mum and everything, but she didn't seem to realise the seriousness of it all."

"Don't worry—she sussed it was you, though."

"Oh good. So do you think she'll have a word with Mum?" asked Laura hopefully.

"I'm sure she will," said Chelsea, thinking that the word in question might not be quite what Laura had in mind. "Anyway," she said, anxious to change the subject, "are you going to tell me why you look like a scarecrow?"

Laura looked down at her mud-stained jeans and grazed hands in surprise. "Oh, yeah, well, I fell off my bike."

"Bad luck," said Chelsea.

"It was wonderful," said Laura, smiling mistily.

"Pardon?" said Chelsea.

"He was so . . . brill."

"Who was?" said Chelsea, wondering whether Laura had banged her head as well as her hands.

"Jon."

"Laura," shouted Chelsea, "can we start this conversation again, please?"

So Laura told Chelsea about the encounter with Jon and after fifteen minutes of hearing about his amazing eyes and fabulous voice and great legs, and how he was even more handsome than Ryan Giggs, Chelsea wished she hadn't asked.

10 Jon Makes a Decision

Jon hadn't really had a clue where he was dashing to when he left Laura gaping at the side of the road. Anywhere, just so long as it was a long way from the continual nagging about homework and studying and being a credit to his father and not letting the side down.

He cycled to the canal, threw his bike down, and slumped under a tree. God, how he hated being an only child. It was like all his father's hopes and fears and ambitions were focused just on him. It had always been the same—he had to live out all his dreams. Ever since he could remember his parents had wanted him to be the first kid in the class to know his times table, the earliest reader, the fastest runner. Why couldn't they let him just be himself?

He knew his dad had wanted to go to university but couldn't because Grandma was a widow and needed Dad to earn money. To Dad, university had always seemed the highest accolade—a sign to the world that you were "someone." He knew his father would be gutted when Jon didn't go—but he'd just have to get used to it.

He sometimes felt that his mum was secretly on his side—but whenever he tried to get her to come out and say what she really felt, she clammed up and told him to do whatever it took to keep his father happy. His mum was really artistic and she seemed bored stiff with the business she ran from a shed—well, studio she called it—in the back garden. She made bouquets and silk posies for weddings, and taught flower arranging and spoke to ladies' lunch clubs and yet somehow she never really seemed excited by what she did. He didn't want to end up like that—doing a job that had no buzz, no excitement to it. His dad went to the office every day and sold houses to people but he never seemed happy. Jon would bet that neither of his parents had ever had a dream of doing anything remotely different, of making a mark on the world. So how could he expect them to understand? Their world was so narrow. It was hopeless.

But he knew one thing for sure. He'd have to tell them what he really wanted to do. He didn't want

to stay at Bellborough Court. He wanted to go to Lee Hill, because there he knew he could do what really interested him.

And tonight, he'd tell them. But after he had been to the disco.

While Jon sat making resolutions by the canal, his mother was setting off to deliver her bouquets. To be honest, she was heartily bored of it—tired of designing bridal posies or making floral hoops for bridesmaids. She was even weary of teaching women with too much time on their hands how to make table centres or entwine ivy round their banisters. She did it because, although Henry hated her to mention it, they needed the money. People weren't buying so many houses right now and Henry's commission had fallen drastically. The money his uncle had left them had almost gone and Jon still had three more years of school at least. So she had to carry on with her job. What she would really like to do was—but no, there was no point thinking about it. She had a duty to Henry and Jon and that was that. She yawned. She was forty-four years old and bored out of her brains.

11 The Hot FM Springs a Surprise

Laura's father, Peter Turnbull, was driving Sonia and Daryl to their swimming lesson and wishing Laura was with him. He had had some good news and wanted to share it with her. In fact, he was in such a good mood that he'd let Sonia tune the car radio to the local station. Normally, Peter liked driving to Mozart or Berlioz, or on a particularly bad day, Mahler, but today he was prepared to be generous, even if that did mean listening to Raving Red. This morning he had heard that Homefinders Inc. had found a buyer for the house in Preston Abbott. What's more, it was a cash buyer. At last he would be able to give Ruth her share of the proceeds and, more important, buy somewhere for himself and Betsy that was big enough for Laura to have a room of her own. That way, she could come to stay far more often.

Mr. Turnbull missed his daughter like crazy. He missed her funny freckled face, the way she turned every minor issue into a three-act drama. He even missed her fiery temper. He saw her most weekends but it wasn't the same as having her with him all the time. Still, she seemed to be handling the whole break-up quite well.

"I've told her she shouldn't carry on like that at her age." Peter pricked up his ears. That voice sounded very familiar.

He turned up the volume.

"I feel sick," said Daryl from the back seat.

"No, you don't," said Peter, who knew that Daryl would try anything to get out of his swimming lesson.

"But I do!" said Daryl.

"Be quiet!" shouted Peter, who like his daughter, was short on the tolerance front. "I'm listening to the radio."

"You said you didn't like the Hot FM," said Sonia from the backseat. "You said it was a load of drivel. And don't shout at my brother," she added. She was allowed to shout at Daryl but she wasn't having this intruder taking liberties.

"But she should be trying to get my dad back, not wrapping herself all round this geek."

"Geek!" Laura's word for everyone from the overweight milkman to her cousin Jeremy. That was Laura's voice! And that was Ginny Gee, Ruth's friend. Well, both their friend once. What was going on? Laura was talking about her mother on the radio. About both of them, in fact. It was Laura, he knew it. He caught a catch in Ginny's voice as she said the caller's name. Ginny knew it too. He turned the volume up again. He had to hear what was going on.

Only he never did. Because at the junction with Western Street and the Drive, Daryl proved irrefutably that he did feel sick.

12 Tempers Fray

"I'm back!" Laura hurled her jacket on to the bottom stair and went into the kitchen.

"I'm surprised you bothered." Her mum did not look happy. Her eyes looked suspiciously pink. Laura swallowed.

"What do you mean?" She opened the cupboard and helped herself to a packet of crisps. Laura always turned to food when she sensed a crisis looming.

"Let me see now—how did it go? 'She is behaving in a really embarrassing way.' Was that it? Oh yes, and 'She shouldn't carry on like that at her age.' Correct me if I'm wrong."

Laura gulped. Her mother never listened to the radio on Saturday mornings. She did the gardening or went shopping. Laura felt dreadful. She never meant to upset her mother, just to sort out this mess in their lives.

"Oh, well, I, er . . . I didn't think you listened to Radio Leehampton."

"No Laura," said her mother, "you simply didn't, think. Period."

"Sorry. Honestly, if I'd known you'd be listening...."

"I don't want to talk about it. Suffice it to say that you are grounded. You are not, repeat not, going to the disco tonight and that is final." Her mum slammed the larder door shut to emphasise her point.

"Why? I mean, why? Everyone's going." Laura looked aghast.

"Correction—everyone but you," said her mother.

"But Sumitha's coming for the night—and you can't spoil her fun even if you try to ruin mine," said Laura angrily. She knew she was in for a punishment, but she couldn't bear the thought of her friends getting to know about it.

"I hadn't got round to phoning the Banerjis to check they approved, and now I won't have to bother. You are not going. And you can tell Sumitha why."

Laura hurled her empty crisp packet across the kitchen. "But I have to—it's The Stomping

Ground's Great Stomp On—there's freebie goodie bags and food and everything. I have to go." Laura's eyes filled with tears.

"Tough." Her mother turned to go.

Laura was seriously worried. Normally her mum was pretty reasonable, but this seemed to have made her truly mad. Because Laura knew deep down it was she who was wrong, and because her weekend was about to be turned into a disaster, she lost her temper.

"God, I hate you!" Laura screamed. "Not content with embarrassing me every time you go out with that jerk, moving into this flea pit of a house, and hardly ever letting me use the phone, you have to ruin what few pleasures I do have. And now you are going to embarrass me in front of Sumitha. She'll probably never speak to me again. But you wouldn't care—you don't give a damn if I am totally friendless and alone."

Her mother turned round. "Laura, for goodness sake, will you stop being so dramatic!"

"I just don't believe you can do this to me. Dad would let me go. But then Dad cares about me. You don't care about anyone but your beloved Melvyn. I HATE YOU!"

Her mother sighed. “Laura—listen to me. That’s simply not true. Of course I care about you. I love you, lots and lots. But you obviously don’t care about me or my feelings. I resent having you broadcasting my private life to half the pubescent population of Leehampton!”

“Oh that’s right—go on, insult my friends, why don’t you? You hate everything else about me, you might as well start hating them, too!” screeched Laura.

“I’m not criticising…”

“Yes you are—you called them pubie phew pooo…”

“PUBESCENT!” said her mother. “It means approaching puberty.”

“Oh.”

“Just think for a moment, Laura. How would you feel if I phoned up some chat show and told the world that my daughter runs a mile at the sight of a spider, spends hours cycling up and down Conway Crescent in hopes of spotting Duncan Nisbet, and is terrified of going upstairs in the dark?”

“That’s different,” mumbled Laura.

“No, it’s not different at all,” said her mother. “I wouldn’t do it because I wouldn’t want to hurt your

feelings. I wouldn't do it because it's no one else's business. But of course, I forget. Mothers are not supposed to have feelings, are they? They are supposed to cook and clean and shop and find the money for kickers and discos and new duvet covers. But feel? Oh no, mothers must never feel anything, must they?" And with that, Laura's mum burst into tears, rushed out of the kitchen, and slammed the door.

Suddenly Laura wished that Moan Line had never been invented.

13 Jemma Writes a Letter

While Laura was feeling very angry and totally unloved and rather guilty, and Ginny Gee was sitting at the traffic lights seething with annoyance at herself for being taken in by her daughter's friend, and Laura's mum was trying to stop her mascara running and wondering why people had kids, Jemma Farrant was sitting cross-legged on her bed writing a letter to her gran.

"Deepdene"
49 Billing Hill
Leehampton LE4 4UP

Dear Gran,
Thank you ever so much for the money you sent me. I've been saving up for this brilliant top from Togs 'n' Clogs and thanks to you, I'll be able to get it today! At the moment I haven't

got a thing worth wearing—just because Mum doesn't care what she wears, she expects me to go around looking like something out of Mothercare's window.

Not that I've got anywhere to go if I did have something. I haven't made any real friends yet, but this girl Laura invited me to go to this place in town—it's called The Stomping Ground and everyone in my class gets to go there on the first Saturday in the month because they have an under-eighteen night. Now Mum says I can't go because she doesn't know what type of people will be there. It's not fair—no other mother makes a fuss like she does.

Can't you make Mum loosen up a bit? I bet you let her do masses of things when she was a kid. Someone like you who cycled to Greece and went swimming in the fountains at Trafalgar Square must have been a really cool mother to have. So why isn't Mum more like you? In biology Mr. Garrett said you got your genes from your parents. What happened with Mum? Was she a changeling? (Joke)

Please come and stay with us soon—I really miss not having someone I can really talk to without having to think about what to say first.

Do write soon.

Loads and loads of luv,

Jemma

Jemma folded the letter and put it in an envelope. She hoped it would work, because if something didn't change soon, she was going to have to take drastic action.

14 The Mums Come to an Agreement

Why, thought Laura's mum, does the phone always ring when you least feel like talking to anyone ever again?

"Leehampton 411266—Ruth Turnbull here."

"Oh, Ruth—it's Claire Farrant, we met outside school last Friday. I'm Jemma's mother, remember?"

Oh yes, the rather frumpy woman in the duffel coat who was worrying about whether there was sufficient supervision of Year Nine swimming and complaining that she had to fetch her daughter because the school bus was so rowdy. What on earth could she want?

"I hope you don't mind my ringing you, only I have a problem," said Mrs. Farrant.

"Well, if I can help," Ruth said politely. Oh, get on with it, woman, she thought.

"It's Jemma. She wants to go to this disco thing at The Stamping Ground tonight."

"Stomping . . ." said Ruth without thinking.

"Pardon?"

"It's The Stomping Ground," clarified Ruth. "But actually . . ."

"Yes, she says your little Laura invited her—so sweet, seeing as Jemma's a bit lonely and doesn't really know many people yet. But to be honest, I'm a bit dubious—you know, only having been here a few weeks, I don't know the place at all. So I said no. Just to be on the safe side. Well, we had histrionics, door slamming, the works. She says Laura often goes. Is that right?"

Ruth hesitated. "Well yes, from time to time but, actually . . ."

"I mean, what sort of reputation has this place got?" continued Claire. "One can't be too careful, can one?" Ruth wondered whether getting out of bed in the morning caused Mrs. Farrant the same amount of anxiety as everything else seemed to.

"Well, apart from bursting eardrums at fifty paces and resembling the Black Hole of Calcutta, it's no worse than any other disco."

Claire sighed. "What sort of youngsters go there?

I mean, Jemma is very immature, and well, she's not used . . . "

"Well, they don't all beat up old ladies and set fire to waste bins here in Leehampton, you know!" Ruth snapped and then gnawed at her lip. It wasn't Claire's fault that the last thing Ruth wanted to talk about was the confounded Stomping Ground. She probably wasn't as neurotic as she sounded. At least there was someone else who was finding that motherhood was not a doddle. She took a deep breath and determined to be cooperative.

"I mean, they have people on the door, and everything, and Friday is under-eighteen night so there's no drink around," she said.

"Oh, well then, I suppose . . . since you're letting Laura go. And apparently, that other girl from their class—Chelsea, is it? The curly-headed one?—she's going. So I thought—if I did the driving there and back—could they all go together? I mean, I'd feel much happier if Jemma was with a friend all the time—and if you approve of the place, well, I'm sure it must be okay!" Mrs. Farrant actually sounded as if she wasn't at all sure that anything was okay.

"Well, the thing is, I had told Laura . . . "

"Oh, I wouldn't expect them to stay late or any-

thing. I'd have them all home by ten-thirty p.m. Earlier, probably. That'd be all right, wouldn't it?"

"Well, actually, I told Laura that she . . . " Ruth ran her fingers distractedly through her hair. "Oh, what the heck—yes, yes that would be fine. Only there'll be another kid from school, Sumitha Banerji, as well. I've got her for the night while her parents go to a dinner dance. Is that okay?"

"Oh, that's no problem. Come to think of it, that name rings a bell—we met someone from the hospital, a colleague of Andrew's, of that name. I wonder if it's the same family. Anyway, it'll be nice for Jemma to get to know someone else," said Claire, pausing momentarily for breath. "Apparently because of the move her social life is at an all-time low."

"Sure you don't mind driving?"

"Not at all. Least I can do. Actually, you've saved my bacon with Jemma. She might start speaking to me again. She thinks I'm the pits at the moment."

"Join the club. See you later."

15
Laura's Reprieve

So much for stern discipline, thought Ruth wryly. But what could she do? Laura had obviously taken Jemma under her wing and it wasn't fair to spoil another kid's evening just because her own was way out of line. The trouble was, Laura would see it as certain victory. Still, it was the easy way out, and right now Mrs. Turnbull didn't have the energy for another argument. These days all her spare time was taken up writing job applications for jobs she didn't want, simply because she needed the money. It seemed no one needed her, she had lost count of the number of "Dear Mrs. Turnbull, Thank you for your application but we regret . . . " letters she had received. Apparently, typing and shorthand were no good these days—you had to be able to understand all these weird computer languages, know what e-mail was, and preferably be able to fax Hong Kong with one hand, while drawing up a spreadsheet with the other. She felt redundant. Still, one person would be pleased with her.

"Laura—come down here a moment, please," she called.

Laura considered not replying but thought that perhaps that was not the best idea.

"Whadyawant?" she muttered, dragging her feet down the stairs.

"Laura, why are you crying?" her mother asked.

"Me? Oh, no reason. After all, why should I cry? Everything is hunky-dory, isn't it? Banned from seeing my friends on the most important night of the entire year. Living in . . . "

"You can go tonight."

"Living in a poky . . . what did you say?"

"I said, you can go tonight."

"Really?"

Her mother sighed. "Really."

"Oh Mum, thanks. I love you, I love you. I do honestly. And I'm sorry about the radio thing. I honestly had your best interests at heart. I didn't mean to hurt your feelings. Oh thanks. What made you change your mind? Can I borrow your cinnamon eye pencil?"

"Jemma Farrant's mum and yes."

"What?"

"Yes, you can borrow . . . "

"No, what about Jemma's mum?"

"She phoned me to say Jemma wanted to go to the disco but because they were new to the town, she was a bit worried. Then she thought that if you and Chelsea were going, Jemma could go with you. Mrs. Farrant is doing the driving—so Mr. Gee won't have to bother. All you are supposed to do is look after Jemma."

"You mean—you actually agreed for Mrs. Farrant to take ME to and from the disco?"

"Yes—why?"

"You mean, she is picking me up? From here?"

"Well, no dear, actually I said you would nip over to her place in the helicopter and land on her roof. Of course she is picking you up from here. Where else would she pick you up from?"

"Anywhere, anywhere but here. Oh, Mum, how could you? What'll I do—I know, Sumitha and I will have to go over to Chelsea's and she can pick us both up there. Mum, how could you suggest she came here? Have you no idea?"

Ruth was puzzled. "Well, I mean, it's hardly out of her way and she did offer."

Laura raised her eyebrows heavenwards at the stupidity of her mother. "Listen Mum, the Farrants live on Billing Hill, in a huge house. Jemma asked me back after school—they've got one of those kitchens like you see in magazines with things hanging down from the ceiling and two bathrooms and a study and everything. They mustn't see this house. No way."

"For God's sake, Laura, you would think we lived in a shanty town. This is a perfectly decent semi-detached house in a perfectly decent close. Just because we used to live in a Victorian eyesore of a place with howling draughts and damp in the cellar you think anything smaller than an aircraft hangar is too downmarket for you."

"Oh, Mum, you don't . . . "

"Understand. I know. Apparently I understand nothing. Well, one thing I do understand is that you set far too much store by outward appearances. Just because, for the time being, we are living in a smaller house than we've been used to, doesn't make us lesser mortals, you know. I have a horrible feeling that you are turning into a little snob. Always worrying about what people will think."

"Well, that's better than being like you and not

caring two hoots about the impression you make or the way you carry on!" shouted Laura.

Don't rise to the bait, Mrs. Turnbull instructed herself. Just count to ten. It didn't do any good so she did it again in French.

"Anyway, you're happy enough to have Sumitha here to stay," she said.

"That's different—her house is small too. Except that her parents are househunting for a bigger house in the country," she added with the air of one who knows that the whole world is better off than her.

"Oh for pity's sake, girl . . . Now do you want to go to this wretched disco or don't you?"

"Yes, yes—thanks Mum. I'll go and ring Chelsea and say I'll wait there for Mrs. Farrant. By the time she brings us home it will be pitch-dark, thank goodness."

16 Jemma's Luck Changes

Jemma was just sealing the envelope when her mother walked in.

"Okay, you win, you can go tonight." Her mother was gnawing her bottom lip, a sure sign that she was not totally happy.

Jemma's mouth dropped open.

"Well, are you going to say something or just stare at me like a goldfish?" asked her mother.

"Thanks, Mum, that's brill." Jemma jumped up and gave her mum a bearlike hug. "But what made you suddenly change your mind?"

"Well, I phoned Laura Turnbull's mother to find out what sort of people went to this Stomping Ground place, and to ask if Laura and Chelsea would go along with you and keep an eye on you so that..."

"You did what?" Jemma whispered.

"I asked Mrs. Turnbull if she approved of the place and when she said it was all right, I said that I would take you and Laura and then she and Chelsea would keep an eye on you."

Oh, that's great, that is, thought Jemma. Thanks, Mum. Thanks a million. Make me look a complete baby, why don't you?

She wanted to yell at her mum and ask her how she thought it looked, having her ring up and check whether somewhere was okay for her to go. She wanted to shout and tell her that by asking them to "look after" her, she was simply making her a laughing stock.

But she said nothing. She bit her tongue and kept quiet. Jemma hated arguments and went out of her way to avoid them. Only it was getting harder. When they had lived in Brighton, Jemma used to go round the corner to Gran's when her parents had an argument—or rather, when Jemma's mum told her dad that no, they were not going to do things that way and if he didn't very much mind, she was the one who would say what was what as far as the kids were concerned—and Gran, who was the most sensible person in the

entire universe, used to give her carrot wine and saffron cake and say it would sort itself out. And it usually did, because Gran would take Mum out for coffee and for a few days after that things would be okay.

Jemma didn't know why her mum made such a baby of her. After all, she had Sam, who if not a baby was after all only six, and she had the twins who were totally babyish at three.

Jemma took a deep breath. "I wish you hadn't said that bit about keeping an eye on me, Mum," she ventured.

Her mother immediately tossed her head, shrugged and looked injured. "Well, really, Jemma, I thought you'd be grateful to me for letting you go. The fact remains, I'm not over the moon about the idea but I decided to meet you halfway. And this is all the thanks I get. If you don't like my conditions, you don't have to go."

"Sorry—thanks. It's really nice of you." Jemma thought fast. At least she was going. "I haven't got anything to wear."

"Oh don't be silly, darling," said her mother, obviously relieved that the confrontation was past. "There's that nice little blue dress with the white collar or your cord skirt and…"

"Don't worry, Mum—I'll find something." And it won't be cord and it won't have a white collar, thought Jemma to herself.

17 Chelsea's Mum Explodes

DEAR GINNY,

GONE TO CORNER SHOP FOR RAISINS FOR LUNCH. CHELSEA UPSTAIRS WITH LAURA, WARWICK GONE TO GARDEN CENTRE. I REMINDED HIM ABOUT HIS JABS AND HE WENT PALE AND LEFT.

BARRY

Ginny staggered to the larder with two carrier bags of groceries and a pained expression. What on earth did he want raisins for? They were having spaghetti bolognese and jam tarts.

Then she caught sight of the dish on the hob. She sniffed. Obviously another one of Barry's creations. He was a good cook, there was no disputing that; it was just that he never remembered that Chelsea and Warwick had very conservative tastes.

Then it hit her. What did the note say? She re-read it. "Chelsea and Laura upstairs." Right, young ladies, she thought, and was about to charge upstairs when her husband ambled through the back door clutching a brown paper bag.

"Good programme, dear?" he asked affably.

"It had its moments," Ginny replied. "What's this about Chelsea and Laura? I thought Chelsea was supposed to help you this morning."

"Help is possibly a slight overstatement. She appeared in the kitchen briefly, moaned about your job for three minutes, and disappeared. She spent most of the morning upstairs with Laura, gassing on the telephone."

"Laura was here this morning?"

"Yes—looked like a demented scarecrow to my mind. They closeted themselves upstairs and yakked as usual." He emptied the raisins on to the work top. "But Laura's gone now—I passed her on my way back."

"Right." Ginny marched to the bottom of the stairs. "Chelsea! Down here! NOW!"

"What's up?" muttered her husband, opening the oven door and putting his gourmet creation on the top shelf.

"I shall kill her," muttered Ginny. Barry withdrew to the garage. He had made his contribution to the smooth running of the household and if Ginny was in a mood, he deemed it safer to be out of the way. He overlooked the small matter of the six dirty saucepans and four plates stacked in the sink. Chelsea shuffled into the kitchen. She had a nasty feeling that she knew what was wrong.

"Chelsea," said her mother, taking a deep breath, and trying to remember all those words of wisdom from Claire Rayner about temper being a sign of weakness, "was Laura in this house this morning when she phoned me on Moan Line? I want a straight answer, yes or no."

"Yes," said Chelsea.

"How COULD you do such a thing?" screeched Ginny, all thoughts of Claire Rayner vanishing in an instant. "Have you any idea how embarrassing that was for me?"

"It wasn't my idea—Laura said . . . "

"I don't give a damn whose IDEA it was. You let her use the phone. She obviously came here with

the express purpose of phoning the programme. Without you egging her on, she'd probably have dropped the whole stupid scheme. And what about Laura's mother—how do you think she's feeling right now?"

"Oh, don't worry, Laura's mum never listens to things like On Your Marks," said Chelsea reassuringly.

"Well, that is where you are wrong, Little Miss Know It All. Ruth told me yesterday that she'd be tuning in because she wanted to hear me. She does happen to be one of my best friends, you know. Or was, until this morning. She probably isn't speaking to me by now."

"Sorry."

"Sorry? Sorry? That's it, is it? You put me in a most embarrassing position, and then all you can say is sorry. I'll have to go and ring Ruth—what she must be thinking, heaven knows. She's got enough on her plate just now without you adding insult to injury. This is just a horrible mess." Ginny ran her fingers through her hair. This didn't cause much trouble as her locks were rigid with fast hold hairspray.

"Well, I didn't ask you to go on the stupid programme, did I?" shouted Chelsea. "You embarrass me every week, writing all that garbage in the paper and wearing stupid clothes that show your knobbly knees and talking about periods on the radio. You go on and on about being 'The Listening Mum with the Ear of the Young' and then you do a meltdown when one of my friends actually wants you to listen. I don't get you at all."

"Listen, it's not . . . Oh blast it, there's the phone. I haven't finished with you yet, young lady."

Ginny snatched up the receiver. "Leehampton 554 . . . "

"Hello? Ginny? It's Ruth." Mrs Turnbull didn't sound very happy.

Ginny took a deep breath. "Oh, hi, Ruth—I was just about to phone you. I, er . . . "

"Doubtless you can guess what I'm phoning about—I . . . " Ruth's voice petered out.

"Look, Ruth, don't," Ginny interrupted. "I'm sorry, really I am. I wouldn't have had that happen for the world, honestly I wouldn't. The thing was, I couldn't block off the call once they'd put it through—and of course, she gave a false name, so I hadn't a clue who it was till I heard her voice. Even then it took me a few minutes to suss her out."

"Oh Ginny, I'm not blaming you—it's that daughter of mine I could cheerfully throttle. And I feel so embarrassed . . ."

"Don't—there's no need, honestly."

Ruth sighed. "Anyone would think, listening to Laura, that I was having a rip-roaring affair and it just isn't like that. Melvyn's a friend—a good friend—but we're not, I mean . . ."

Ginny murmured soothingly, wondering whether Barry's lunch was meant to smell so strange. Why couldn't he have just made spaghetti bolognese?

"And what'll Peter think? We were just beginning to be friends again."

"Oh, he won't have been listening to teenage junk like that," said Ginny reassuringly.

"I hope not. Except that those kids of Betsy's have the radio on all the time, apparently. Still, knowing him he won't have sussed anything. Oh, why did she have to do it, Ginny? Why didn't she just talk to me?" Ruth sounded near to tears.

Ginny sighed. "Because she's an adolescent, because she thinks she knows everything, because she believes you know nothing—in short because she's an irritating, self-important, thoroughly normal teenager."

"And what will her friends think of me? Worse, what will her friends' parents think? They'll see me as some sort of hussy, they'll . . ."

"Stop it, Ruth," interrupted Ginny. "Listen. First, how many parents do you think would have been listening? Answer—hardly any. Second, of those listening, how many would recognise Laura's voice, remember, she called herself Becky. They will all have been too busy vacuuming carpets and cleaning cars and yelling at their own kids to worry about some child on the radio with a moan about her mother."

Ruth laughed weakly. "I suppose so. I suppose I'm doing what Laura does all the time—making a mountain out of a molehill and turning a drama into a crisis! Anyway, I told Laura she couldn't go to the disco tonight—I thought it was time I came down hard. Showed her who was boss."

"Quite right, too. I'll do the same with Chelsea," said Ginny.

"No, wait," interrupted Ruth. "I'd just decided—and then Claire Farrant phoned—she's the mother of that new girl, Jemma . . . "

"Oh yes, I know—her husband's the new consultant at the General—we did a profile on him in the

paper last month," said Ginny.

"Well, she said that she would only let Jemma go if she went with Laura and Chelsea. So—what could I do? I relented. Now Madam will probably think I'm a soft touch—oh, and by the way, Claire's driving. You can give Barry the night off! Oh, and Laura wants to come to your house to wait for the lift," continued Mrs. Turnbull. "Apparently Wordsworth Close is beyond the pale."

Ginny groaned. "Honestly, kids! Who'd have 'em? Er, Ruth . . . "

"Yes?"

"We are still friends, aren't we?"

"Of course we are."

"Good."

Chelsea, who had been leaning over the banister eavesdropping on her mother's conversation, heaved a sigh of relief. She hadn't been banned from the disco.

"CHELSEA!"

Well, not yet anyway.

She scurried back into the kitchen. Her mother was wielding a dirty saucepan. "Can't you ever do anything to help?" she shouted. "There are dishes

in the sink, bits of egg yolk on the countertops—you might at least have cleared things up while I was sorting out the mess you made with my friendships."

Chelsea thought it best not to question her mother's reasoning. It wasn't she who had cooked some South American garbage for lunch. Why couldn't her dad do it? However, under the circumstances, it might be a good idea, she thought, to do something helpful with a cloth.

18 Sumitha Gets Through Stage One

Over on Wellington Road, Sumitha was counting the minutes until her parents left for their night away.

"Now Sumitha, behave yourself while we're gone," said Mr. Banerji, as he meticulously packed the boot of the car. He was a man who paid great attention to detail, from the mirror shine on his black shoes to exact timing of the number of minutes his daughter spent on her French homework.

"Yes, Dad," said Sumitha, wondering what her father would say if he knew what she was really planning.

"We'll drop you off on the way, and then I can see Mrs. Turnbull before we go," said Sumitha's mother. "Get your things, dear."

Sumitha's heart sank. If they dropped her off,

something was bound to be said about the disco.

"We don't have time, Chitrita," said her father. "We are running late already."

"But, Rajiv, it will look so rude..." began Mrs. Banerji, adjusting the jade and gold sari she had bought for the occasion.

"It's okay, Mum," said Sumitha. "Why don't you just drop me at the end of their road. I'll say hi to Mrs. Turnbull for you and explain that you had to dash."

"Well, if you are sure..."

"Chitrita, we must get a move on." Sumitha's father was not one to be kept waiting.

All the way to Wordsworth Close, Sumitha's father and mother gave instructions. "Say please and thank you. Offer to help with the clearing up. Don't leave wet towels in the bathroom." And all the way Sumitha said yes and no in what she hoped were all the right places.

As she waved good-bye to the disappearing car, Sumitha heaved a sigh of relief. For one awful moment, she had thought her plans would be destroyed. If they had gone to Laura's house, and if Laura's mother had said anything about the disco...

She rang the bell. "Hello, dear," said Laura's

mother, "are your parents not coming in?"

"No, Mrs. Turnbull, they had to dash off," said Sumitha. "They asked me to say thank you for them." Sumitha gave her one of her winning smiles.

"Oh dear, and I was going to check with them that it was all right for you to go to the disco tonight." Mrs. Turnbull looked anxiously down the road.

"Oh yes," said Sumitha. "I've got my stuff in the bag." She held up her Naf Naf rucksack.

Well, she didn't say they knew about the stuff in the bag, did she, she reasoned with herself. Just that she had it with her.

"Oh good," said Laura's mum. "Laura! Sumitha's here."

Laura appeared from the hallway. "Everything okay?" she asked with a knowing look.

"Great," said Sumitha. "Just great." They taught you at drama class to keep a straight face. It was proving a useful attribute.

19 Mr. Turnbull Thinks Things Through

Laura's dad had driven out to the old house at Preston Abbott to take one last look. Betsy was at home looking after a pallid Daryl and Sonia had gone bowling with her friends. Peter had been thinking a lot about the past and wanted to see the house once more. It looked even more of a monstrosity now than it had when they lived there, he thought. Of course, it had been a crazy house to buy—it had stood empty for two years before they found it, which was why they had got it so cheap. It had once been a vicarage, in the days when the clergy lived in style, and he and Ruth had had great ideas about doing it up, restoring it to its former glory, and filling it with antiques.

They soon discovered that big rooms look nice but cost a bomb to heat, and old houses harbour damp and woodworm. They spent all their money just keeping warm and repairing the roof, and in the end they began to hate the house for taking up all their time and most of their money. They stopped having holidays and bought drainpipes instead, and every winter they did battle with the ancient boiler and moved all the furniture as close to the fire as they could.

When he and Ruth decided to split up, the one thing neither of them was sad about was leaving the house. But Laura was devastated. The Old Vicarage suited her sense of style and her love of the dramatic. She told everyone they had a resident ghost, and sat for hours in the dilapidated summer house writing stories about imaginary families who lived there in the past. She always gave her address as The Old Vicarage, Preston Abbott, when in fact it was The Old Vicarage, 26 Woodland Lane, Preston Abbott.

"Don't put the road in, Dad," she said when he had some letterheads printed. "It looks much more uppercrust without."

Peter chuckled to himself. Laura was like that—always wanting things to look just right. She told her friends he was an international financier, when in fact he worked as an accountant with an

import/export company. When they had spent ten days camping in the Loire Valley, she told people that they were “visiting a friend’s château.” She was, he feared, something of a snob. But a very loveable little snob.

He did hope she was happy. He had been sure of it—she was always chattering nineteen to the dozen when he had her for the day, and when she phoned him, he couldn’t get a word in edgeways. But then occasionally, he wondered. Like this morning. He couldn’t get the radio programme out of his head. If only Daryl hadn’t decided to throw up all over the car he would have heard the rest. It sounded as if Ruth had got a new man friend. Well, good for her—it would help Peter feel less guilty if he knew she was happy. Only Laura obviously had a problem, and that bothered him. Perhaps he should phone tonight. Yes, that was it—he’d phone and talk to Laura and find out what was what.

20
Jemma Covers Up

Jemma glowered at her reflection in the mirror and yanked the elastic band off her ponytail. Should she put her hair up now? She had been copying a picture in *Yell!* magazine and reckoned it made her look much older. But if she went downstairs with a French plait, her mother would only have a purple fit and then everything else might be revealed. She'd just have to do it at the disco.

"Come along, Jemma love, time to go." Mrs. Farrant's voice floated up the stairs.

Jemma took a deep breath. This was it. She really had to make a good impression tonight. Making friends when you turn up at a new school in the middle of the term isn't easy at the best of times, and when you have a mother who insists on treating you as if you were at infant school instead of practically fourteen, who puts dinosaur biscuits in your lunch box, and who delights in making you a laughing stock in front of the entire world, it's even harder. But Laura Turnbull had been really nice to her, and when she had invited her to The Stomping Ground, Jemma couldn't believe her luck. She wasn't about to blow things now.

She slipped the mascara, eye shadow, and lipstick she had bought that morning (when she was supposed to be getting toothpaste and bubble bath) into her anorak pocket and pulled the zip right up to the neck to hide her clothes. She hated this childish anorak, but for once it served a purpose. She slipped the silver slingbacks she had "borrowed" from the back of her mother's wardrobe into her bag. Her mum wouldn't notice. She never wore them; she never wore anything remotely stylish. With a bit of luck, Jemma just might get away with it.

"Now listen, Jemma petal," began Mrs. Farrant as she manoeuvred the car out of the driveway and on to Billing Hill, "don't accept anything from anyone tonight, not sweets, not drinks . . . "

"Oh Mum, stop it—I'm not a baby," sighed Jemma. "I'm only going to a disco—not into a den of sleaze, you know."

"Yes, well, you can't be too careful," said her mother. "Now, are you sure you've got everything? Money for the phone, comb? Will you be warm enough? It's still very chilly at night. What have you got on under there?"

"Er, oh, my cream shirt," said Jemma hastily, crossing her fingers behind her back.

"Oh, lovely, pet—the one I got you from Kids' Stuff. Very pretty."

"I think we are just coming up to Chelsea's turning now," said Jemma quickly, in order to change the subject. "She said it was first left past the church."

"All right, love," said Mrs. Farrant, pulling up outside Number 19. "I'll just pop in and collect your friends."

"MUM! Just toot the horn!"

Mrs. Farrant sighed. "Darling, tooting horns is very rude. I'll reverse into their drive and you can go to the door."

There was a teeth-jarring crunch as Mrs. Farrant attempted to get into reverse. A laurel bush shuddered as the rear wheel careered into a flower bed.

"Oh Mum," sighed Jemma, "stay where you are. Just don't do anything. Just sit there."

21 Finishing Touches

While Jemma was attempting to sort her mother out, Chelsea, Sumitha, and Laura were putting the finishing touches to their ensembles.

"You're sure I look okay? You don't think this top makes me look too fat? What about my zit? Does it show?" Chelsea frowned in the mirror.

"You look great, honestly," said Laura, who was staring wide-eyed into the bathroom mirror with her tongue sticking out as she tried to draw an even line with her mum's Seductive Cinnamon eyeliner.

"What shall I do with my hair?" wailed Sumitha. "Oh, I wish I could have it all cut off. I hate it." She shook her head and flicked her long black hair behind her back.

"You're lucky," said Chelsea, "you could put yours up. Mine's at the grotty in-between stage and it goes frizzy all the time. I don't think it will ever grow any longer." She shook her curly locks in disgust.

"At least yours is a decent colour," said Laura to Chelsea. "Ginger is just the pits—have you ever seen a supermodel with ginger hair?"

"But you want to be a novelist, not a supermodel," reasoned Chelsea.

"That," said Laura, "is not the point."

"Anyway, auburn hair is a sign of creativity," said Sumitha knowledgeably. "Loads of poets have auburn hair."

Laura felt better.

"What do you think Jemma will wear?" she said, pouting her lips and applying copious layers of Sunburnt Rust. "Her mother's really old-fashioned about clothes and makeup and stuff."

"She seems a bit of a goody-goody—Jemma, I mean," said Chelsea. "She's really babyish. I know she's the youngest in the year, and she's new and everything, but she's a bit wet. I don't think she'd say boo to a goose without someone holding her hand. Why did you go and invite her?"

"Oh, I don't know," said Laura. "I felt sorry for her, I suppose. She doesn't know anyone and that day when her mum turned up at the classroom door

to fetch her, she looked so embarrassed. I mean, imagine having your mum do something like that. Those awful maroon tights she had on!" They all tittered.

"Not to mention that rain hat," giggled Chelsea.

"Girls, Mrs. Farrant's here." Ginny called up the stairs.

Sumitha stood stock still. "Isn't your mum driving us?" she said to Chelsea.

"Nope. Mrs. Farrant wants us to hold little Jemma's hand." She pulled a face. "And in exchange, she gets to do the driving."

"Oh no," gasped Sumitha. "I thought we'd be meeting Jemma there."

"Well, what difference does it makes who takes us, as long as we get there?" said Laura.

"But Mr. Farrant is the new ear, nose, and throat surgeon at the hospital where my dad works," said Sumitha. "Dad does all his X-rays and stuff, and if Dad gets to hear about tonight . . . "

"Oh, he won't," said Chelsea, throwing on her black leather jacket and running one last blob of gel through her hair. "Fathers never talk about things like that. Come to think of it, Jemma's dad probably hasn't got a clue that there's a disco on. Mine lives in a world of his own," she added reassuringly.

"I suppose so." Sumitha did not sound convinced.

"Girls! Come on—don't keep Mrs. Farrant waiting!" Ginny sounded irritated.

They clattered downstairs.

"Now, Chelsea, remember what I told you," began Ginny. "No smoking, no accepting anything from . . ."

"Oh Mum, don't go on—you're not on the radio now."

"I'm just reminding you," said Ginny calmly. "Better safe than sorry. Have a great time, girls—see you later."

Chelsea and Laura piled into the back of Mrs. Farrant's Polo, giving one another a sidelong glance at the sight of Jemma in her lime green and lilac anorak buttoned up to the neck. They couldn't been seen hanging round the disco with someone like her! They'd have to lose her once they were inside.

"Hi," said Jemma. She looked anxious.

"Hi," they said.

The inside of the car was boiling hot. This was because Mrs. Farrant kept mistaking the tempera-

ture regulator for the windscreen wiper button. Chelsea and Laura unbuttoned their jackets. Jemma looked purple in the face, but still remained buttoned up.

"My goodness, Chelsea dear, that is a short little jumper, isn't it?" said Mrs. Farrant. "Won't you be frightfully chilly later on?"

"Mum . . . " hissed Jemma, sinking further into her anorak in mortification.

"It's a cropped top, Mrs. Farrant," smiled Chelsea sweetly. "It's the in thing right now."

"It's very revealing, isn't it?" replied Jemma's mum, peering through the driving mirror and swerving rather violently into the middle of the road. An oncoming lorry driver made a gesture which indicated what he thought of middle-aged women drivers.

Mrs. Farrant was rather surprised at all the girls—they were wearing a great deal of makeup. She was glad that Jemma wasn't like that—she always thought it was such a pity when children grew up too soon. She peered through the mirror again and narrowly missed the kerb.

"Mum . . . "

Jemma found her mother's driving only marginally less of an embarrassment than her fondness for frilly blouses and white ankle socks. She had failed her test four times before passing, and only persevered because Mr. Farrant was always too busy at the hospital to take the twins to playgroup or Sam to his swimming lessons.

Fortunately, Mrs. Farrant was not too sure of the way to The Stomping Ground and the rest of the journey passed without further comment on the fashion leanings of her passengers. After three wrong turns, two circuits of the St Andrews roundabout and a brief trip the wrong way up a one-way street, they arrived.

"Now, petals, you three will keep an eye on Jemma . . . "

"MUM!" Jemma slammed the car door and headed for the entrance. The others offered beatific smiles and obedient nods to her mother and made a dash for the disco.

They were all secretly thinking that despite the mothers they had been landed with, they could have done a lot worse. At least theirs, at their very worst, never called them petal.

22
Feeling the Heat

By half past eight, Jemma was feeling well satisfied. She'd grabbed hold of Laura's arm the moment they arrived and dashed to the loo.

"What's up—are you ill?" gasped Laura, hoping that Jemma wasn't going to be a perfect bind.

"No, I just need your help," said Jemma, and she produced her makeup and her mum's silver slingbacks. Laura eyed them in undisguised envy.

Between them, they had made up her eyes like it showed you in *Shriek!* ("Look alluring yet remote"), applied a liberal dousing of Anaïs Anaïs perfume, which Jemma's gran had given her for Christmas, and scraped her hair up into a sort of scrunchy bun on the top of her head with the help of half a can of hairspray.

Jemma's reward had been instant.

"You look amazing," Chelsea had said as Jemma strolled—well, tottered—into the disco.

"Wow, Jemma, you look so—different!" Sumitha had gasped when she saw her.

"That top is fantastic!" said Laura, eyeing Jemma's velvet body admiringly. "Where did you get it?"

"At Chic," said Jemma. "My gran sent me some money and I told mum I was saving for a cardigan, but got this instead!"

"It's mega," said Sumitha. "And I'd die for those shoes."

They seemed to approve. All was well in Jemma's world. The fact that her eyes kept sticking together (perhaps she had used a tad too much mascara) and she was itching like crazy all over her forehead was a small price to pay for being one of the gang.

By half past eight Laura was in seventh heaven. She had been sipping a Diet Coke when she saw him sauntering through the door with another boy. It was Jon. Her hands went all clammy and her heart began doing extraordinary things in the region of her tonsils.

"That's him!" she muttered to Chelsea out of the corner of her mouth.

"What's who?" said Chelsea.

"Over there—DON'T LOOK NOW!—it's Jon!

The one I told you about. DON'T LOOK! Isn't he gorgeous?"

"If I can't look, how can I tell whether he's gorgeous or not?" asked Chelsea reasonably.

"Oh my God, he's coming this way! What shall I do? What shall I say? Oh . . . "

Jon ambled past Laura, apparently deep in conversation with his mate.

"Hi," she whispered.

Jon didn't notice her.

By eight thirty-five Sumitha was still having difficulty believing her luck. It had worked. She was here. Of course, telling Laura's mum that her parents were perfectly happy for her to go was a bit naughty, but then what they didn't know couldn't hurt them. And they'd never find out. Would they? Well, if they did, she'd have to face the music when it happened. At least she would have had her fun and they couldn't take that away from her.

"Keep moving," Jon hissed at Rob as they made their way to the snack bar.

"What?"

"Just move over there, now!" said Jon.

Rob moved—ably assisted by Jon's kneecap in his back.

"It's that girl I told you about, the one I had the prang with this morning," he muttered.

He could see her staring at him with those big green eyes. She had a strange look on her face. It was somehow disconcerting, that look. Jon turned to Rob, but he had disappeared on to the dance floor with a girl from his school.

"Wanna dance?" he muttered to the girl on his left and grabbed her arm. Anything to avoid Laura. The memory of the morning's encounter still made him squirm. He must have looked a right idiot bombing down the drive like that, and she hadn't exactly been backward in telling him what she thought. She was probably dying to point him out to all her mates and tell them what a dork he had been.

"Wanna dance?" he repeated, turning to look at the owner of the arm he had grabbed.

Sumitha couldn't believe her luck. Freedom and a boy to dance with all in one evening.

By quarter to nine Chelsea was enjoying herself. She thought Rob was quite sexy-looking. He was a

year above her at school, but she had seen him playing soccer a few times and found his thighs quite mesmerising. Perhaps this was it. Perhaps this would be her first proper love affair. She closed her eyes and swayed to the music. Rob trod on her toe.

By nine o'clock Ginny Gee was mortified. She had decided to defrost the fridge and there, in a soggy heap under a packet of week-old radishes that looked as if it were growing penicillin, she had found Chelsea's poem.

"Barry," she said, taking it into the sitting room. "Barry," she repeated. "BARRY!" she yelled. Her beloved raised his eyes in slow motion from the *Times Two* crossword.

"Mmmm," he murmured.

"Read this!" She threw the damp paper at him. He squinted.

He chuckled. He sipped his coffee and tittered. Then he guffawed. "Oh, that's good, isn't it? Oh yes very good indeed. One of Chelsea's masterpieces, is it? Oh yes, I like that!"

"Oh, so you think it's funny, do you?" shouted his wife. "And I suppose you find my dress sense a source of great mirth and merriment as well?"

Barry tried to put on a straight face. And failed. "Well, you must admit, love, you do go a bit over the top at times. You are not as young as you used to be and . . ."

Barry spent the next twenty minutes attempting to remove coffee stains from his jeans.

Ginny spent the next thirty minutes in front of the wardrobe mirror, wondering whether, after all, she was quite such a fashion icon as she thought she was.

Barry wondered whether he would ever learn. He adored his bouncy wife but sometimes she was just a bit exhausting. And she did hate growing older. It was hard work sometimes keeping up with her. But he did love her and he never meant to upset her. He thought he had better go and make peace.

At nine-twenty the phone rang in Mrs. Turnbull's house. It was Peter.

"Oh, hi," said Ruth tentatively. "I'll just take the call upstairs." Melvyn was in the sitting room mending her table lamp and somehow she didn't feel able to talk naturally to Peter if he was listening.

"Well, I really wanted a word with Laura," said

Mr. Turnbull when she picked up the bedroom extension.

"She's out at a disco," said Ruth, for some reason disappointed that it wasn't her he wanted to chat to.

"Oh. Well, er—I mean, she is okay, isn't she? Happy, and all that?" He sounded hesitant.

Oh no. He'd heard it. The Hot FM. She knew it.

"Yes, she's fine," she said. "Why?"

"Oh nothing, no reason. I just wondered . . . "

"You heard it, didn't you, Peter?" Ruth decided to get it over and done with. "You heard that phone-in thing when Laura pretended to be someone else?"

"Well, a bit of it, yes. Till Daryl was sick all over the gear stick, that is."

Mrs. Turnbull chuckled despite herself. Peter had never been very good with blood or vomit.

"Listen, Peter, it's not what you think—I mean, the thing is . . . oh, look, it's difficult to talk right now." She could hear Melvyn coming upstairs. He did tend to follow her around like a lost puppy.

"Is this new man—sorry, geek," he laughed, "is he with you?"

"Well, yes, but he only popped in to mend my

lamp, I mean he isn't . . . "

"Look, Ruth, I don't mind. I'm pleased for you. I've got Betsy and I am glad you've found someone. All I'm concerned about is Laura."

"Laura's fine—just a bit overdramatic at times," she said shortly.

"Great—well, I'll see her soon then. Ciao."

Mrs. Turnbull put the phone down.

"So much for thinking he'd be upset about my love life," she muttered to herself.

23 The Witching Hour

By ten o'clock Laura was in the slough of despond. She'd watched Jon dancing with Sumitha, with Chelsea, even once with Jemma, but not with her. Every time she managed to catch his eye, he looked away. He hadn't spoken a single syllable to her, not even when she had accidentally-on-purpose knocked into him when she went to get her pizza. It was because the others looked really good—Sumitha with her pixie face, gorgeous hair and china-doll figure, Chelsea with that great smile and bags of confidence. Even Jemma looked a million dollars tonight. If only she'd been wearing something half decent, she knew he would have noticed her. It was all her mum's fault. She was never going to get a boyfriend at this rate.

"What's the matter?" Jemma asked her kindly. "You look a bit miserable."

So Laura told Jemma about Jon and the bike and

the fact that she really thought he was dishy. And Jemma said, "He lives next door to us," in the sort of voice people use to tell you there are roadworks on the M1.

"Next door? To you?" Laura stuttered.

"Yes. His mum brought us in a cake the day we moved in, and my mum's getting her to make some flower arrangements for our hall. Jon goes to Bellborough Court—I see him at the bus stop every day."

Life, thought Laura, was grossly unfair. She would definitely have to keep up her friendship with Jemma. It could prove extremely useful.

By ten o'clock Chelsea was starry-eyed. She'd got on really well with Rob, dancing and chatting and—once—even kissing. Well, a hurried peck really, but she could embroider it a bit for school on Monday. Then he'd actually asked her what her surname was, and where she lived and stuff, and she thought, I've cracked it, he's going to ask me out.

"Gee? I don't suppose you are anything to do with Ginny Gee from the radio? The one who writes for the *Echo?*" he asked.

Chelsea grunted noncommitally.

"Pardon?" said Rob.

"Well, actually, she's my mother," said Chelsea.

"Mega," said Rob. "Wow, fancy having a celeb as a mum. I never knew you were her daughter. She's a really funny writer. My mum creases at her stuff."

"Oh yeah?" said Chelsea.

They danced about a bit more. Chelsea tried desperately to think of something immensely witty to say.

"Can I come round to see you tomorrow?" Rob asked suddenly.

"Yes, oh yes," said Chelsea breathily.

"Great—what time?"

"Any time, any time at all," murmured Chelsea.

Rob held her close. Chelsea was in heaven.

By ten o'clock, Sumitha was getting worried. Jemma's mum would be here to pick them up in a bit and Jon was still dancing with her. Really close. It was great. He was really nice and a pretty hot dancer, too. But Sumitha couldn't risk Mrs. Farrant seeing her with Jon. Not if there was any chance Dad would get to hear of it. And from the little she had seen of Mrs. Farrant, she could quite believe that she would spill the beans.

"Um, er, excuse me," she said to Jon, "I have to go to the loo," and dashed off the floor and through the swing door to the Ladies.

By quarter past ten Jemma was in agony. The silver slingbacks had made huge blisters on her feet, and she was having some sort of weird allergic reaction to the makeup; her cheeks felt hot and itchy and her eyes kept watering. But she was happy. She'd danced a lot and talked to loads of people. Any minute now, though, her mum would be here—she was always early—and she had to get the makeup off her face and get Chelsea and Laura and Sumitha out on to the pavement. She couldn't risk being banned from coming again, just because they weren't ready in time. She headed for the Ladies and a quick switch back to Jemma Farrant, obedient daughter in an anorak.

Jon had had a good evening. He'd managed to dodge Laura, even though he could feel her eyes boring right through him. She'd probably told everyone about this morning. But he'd had a great time with Sumitha. She was a lot more interesting than most of the girls he tried to chat up. And yet,

he hadn't actually chatted her up. He'd found himself telling her all about his dad and how he wanted him to go to university, and Sumitha had told Jon how her dad wouldn't let her do the things her friends did. And then she had asked him what he wanted to do and he'd told her. And she hadn't laughed. She had asked lots of questions and said that she thought he should go for it. And he'd said she should just go and get her hair cut and then her dad wouldn't be able to do anything. "Except wait for it to grow back," Sumitha had said. And they'd laughed. It had been a really good night.

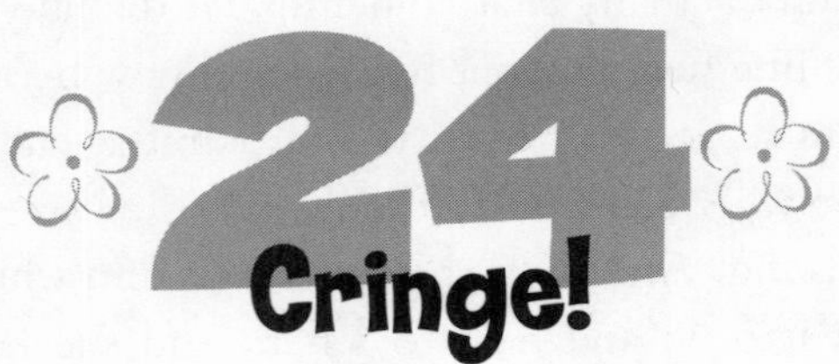

24 Cringe!

"OH NO, IT'S MY MUM!" Jemma stopped dead in her tracks coming out of the Ladies. Standing in the middle of the dance floor, wearing a flared corduroy skirt, blue tights, Hush Puppies and a worried expression, was Mrs. Farrant.

"Chelsea, Laura—hello, darlings, home time!" she shrilled, shielding her eyes against the flashing lights. "Where's Jemma got to?" Jemma froze. She wanted the ground to open and swallow her up. What was Mum thinking of, coming in here, embarrassing her in front of all these people? Everyone knew that it just wasn't done—parents waited outside. No one else's mother would have been so thick. Hadn't she any idea of how to behave in public? She had told her in words of one syllable to wait outside.

She watched as Chelsea and Laura stopped in midtwirl and fought a losing battle with a fit of mild hysterics. Several other kids were nudging one another and laughing behind their hands. Jemma wanted to die.

"My," she heard her say, "what's all this racket then, girls?"

"Jungle music," Chelsea replied, somewhat tersely. "I'll go and find Jemma for you," she added much louder, hoping that everyone who was watching would realise that this woman was nothing to do with her.

Jemma took a deep breath. "It's okay, Chelsea, I'm here." She walked over to her mum.

"Mum, why didn't you wait outside?" she hissed. "Everyone's looking at you. Go outside. NOW!"

"Sorry, petal, but . . . "

"Don't call me petal," snapped Jemma.

" . . . but I couldn't find a parking space big enough so I'm up in The Mounts car park. Come along, now, everyone. Where's little Sumitha? Oh there she . . . er, who is that she's, er, with—oh my goodness!"

Jemma's mother was standing, openmouthed, giving a highly effective imitation of a gobsmacked goldfish.

"Isn't that Jon Joseph from next door?"

"Yes," mumbled Laura, who having suffered all evening watching Sumitha dancing so expertly, was not overjoyed at seeing her saying farewell to Jon in what seemed an unnecessarily friendly manner.

Mrs. Farrant's unceasing chatter dwindled to a sort of strangled gasp. Little Sumitha Banerji, daughter of that nice Rajiv Banerji from Radiology, the one they'd sat next to at the League of Friends' Midsummer Ball, was entwined with Jon, Anona's boy. Very closely. In fact, thought Mrs. F, you could hardly see where Jon ended and Sumitha Banerji began.

"Sumitha dear! Over here now, please," she called.

"Oh Mum—don't!" groaned Jemma. Chelsea and Laura had already dived out on to the pavement in horror.

Sumitha gulped. She hadn't realised that Mrs. Farrant had arrived. She had thought she would just have time to say good-bye to Jon before she went outside. Seeing the expression on Mrs. Farrant's face, Sumitha felt slightly sick.

Claire Farrant was very surprised to see Sumitha being so, well, familiar with Jon. She would have thought that the Banerjis would have drawn the line at that sort of thing. After all, she was still only a child. Still, some parents had no control. Jemma was lucky to have a caring mother who had her best interests at heart. She shepherded her charges to the door, wondering why they were hanging their heads and looking for all the world as if they wanted to be a million miles away.

"What HAVE you got on, young lady?" said Jemma's mum suddenly, catching sight of her daughter's attire. In her mortification, Jemma had forgotten to zip up the anorak. It didn't matter. Who cared? Her life was over anyway.

25 Moments of Reckoning

You could cut the air with a knife in Mrs. Farrant's Polo. Jemma was in the front seat, cringing with embarrassment and fighting back tears of frustration. Mrs. Farrant was sitting bolt upright, gripping the steering wheel and holding forth about growing up before your time and looking cheap and nasty and sending out all the wrong signals and mixing with the wrong type of people. The others were in the back: Chelsea was trying very hard to keep a straight face and wondering whether she was the one who was supposed to be the wrong type of person; Laura was gazing out of the window, thinking about Jon and hating Sumitha for having monopolised him all evening. He was her friend, not Sumitha's. (Laura overlooked the fact that knocking someone off their bike and speaking all of half a dozen sentences to them did not really give one full rights of possession.)

Meanwhile, Sumitha was praying very hard to every god she had ever heard of and several she hadn't. *Please, please, please don't let Dad find out.*

"Thank you so much for fetching us, Mrs. Farrant," said Chelsea, hoping to pacify the irate woman with her charming manners.

Mrs. Farrant crunched her gears.

"Yes, it was very kind of you," added Laura. "It was a great evening, wasn't it, Jemma?"

"It was brilliant," added Sumitha. "I had a really good time." Till now, she added silently.

"We noticed," muttered Laura.

Sumitha appeared not to hear.

"How long have you known Jon Joseph, Sumitha?" asked Mrs. Farrant as she went round the roundabout for the second time, having missed her turning.

Sumitha gulped. This was tricky. Mrs. Farrant obviously knew Jon. Mr. Farrant also knew Dad. "Oh, he's a family friend, Mrs. Farrant," she said. "We haven't seen him in ages—it was nice catching up with him again." She crossed her fingers under her jacket.

"Oh I see," said Mrs. Farrant doubtfully. "Well, that's nice, dear."

I think I've got away with it, thought Sumitha. There is a god after all.

At last they drew up outside Laura's house. "I'll just see you two to the door, Laura," said Mrs. Farrant.

"Oh no, please don't bother," said Laura hastily. "We'll be fine." There was no way she wanted Mrs. Farrant noting the peeling paint on the front porch or the fact that the doorbell was stuck over with sticking plaster because it didn't work and her mother kept forgetting to buy a new battery.

And then it happened. The front door opened. Mrs. Turnbull gave a cheery wave. She was clad in her blue velvet housecoat with the white patch where Laura had knocked the bleach over it. She had bare feet. She had taken her makeup off and her nose was shiny. But worst of all, standing beside her with a stupid grin on his face was the oik Melvyn. Laura cringed. How could she do it? Had she no pride? Standing there in full view of the entire neighbourhood flaunting her boyfriend. Laura couldn't bear it.

"Thanks so much, Claire," Mrs. Turnbull called. "I'll do the same for you next time."

"I am not sure that there will be a next time for

Jemma," said Mrs. Farrant, tersely. "I think perhaps I was wrong to let her go after all. She seems to have been somewhat led astray. I'll be in touch."

And she drove off, hitting the kerb as she went. As she shut the front door, Laura saw Chelsea and Jemma eyeing Melvyn with interest. She thought she would probably just go upstairs, lie down, and die.

"What was all that about?" asked her mother. She looked weary.

Laura shrugged. "Dunno," she said "Are you going?" she said pointedly to Melvyn.

"Yes, 'fraid so—just off, honeybunch."

Laura gritted her teeth. "We're just going to make some hot chocolate, Mum," said Laura. Anything to avoid Sumitha witnessing her mother slobbering farewell to that slime-bag.

26
The Post Mortem

"Mum! How could you? You ruined everything!" Jemma was in tears. "It had been such a good evening and then you came in and…"

"Oh, a good evening, was it?" snapped her mother, slamming the front door. "Your idea of a good evening is disporting yourself in cheap and tacky clothes and smearing makeup all over your face. Not to mention stealing my shoes, which are probably ruined. I've had those since my wedding day. Of course, I blame your new friends. You'd never have done a thing like that until we moved here. And you told me they were such nice girls."

"They ARE nice," shouted Jemma. "Very nice."

"Well, I don't know what their mothers are thinking of, letting them go out looking like that. I mean it's . . . "

"Their mothers are thinking of them, that's what!" sobbed Jemma. "You just haven't got a clue, have you? Their mothers want them to have a good time, to be with their friends. Their mothers don't spend their whole lives trying to ruin their kids' chances of ever having a life."

"Jemma, please!" Mrs. Farrant put her hand on Jemma's shoulder. Jemma wrenched it away.

"Well, it's true. You never let me grow up. You say you want me to have friends, but then you try and keep me a baby. You're always finding reasons why not to do things and you won't even buy me fashionable gear—even Gran says that my clothes lack imagination," cried Jemma.

"Oh well, she would, she's always been weird," retorted her mother.

"Well, I'd rather have weird than prehistoric! Just because you go around looking like a country bumpkin, why do I have to suffer? You take me shopping and expect me to have stupid kids' clothes, you won't let me wear makeup. If you don't like what I was wearing, then it's your own fault. If you bought me decent stuff, I wouldn't have to go behind your back, would I? So don't blame me!"

"Now look here, Jemma, don't you speak to me like that. I only have your best interests at heart," insisted Mrs. Farrant.

But Jemma, who had bottled up her feelings for so long, was now in full flood.

"No, you haven't!" she sobbed. "All you want is to boss us all around—choose our clothes, tell us when to go to bed, iron our knickers. Well, do it for the twins and leave me alone!"

And with that Jemma stormed out of the kitchen and slammed the door. Her mother sat down on the kitchen stool and started to think. Jemma had never gone on like this about clothes before. In fact, Jemma had always been a very easy-going child. She did hope that this new school wasn't having a bad effect on her.

Laura started to boil the milk. Her mother, who had been surprisingly quick at getting rid of Melvyn, came and removed the pan from her hand. "Sit," she said. "And you, Sumitha."

They sat.

"Your mother phoned a while back, Sumitha," said Ruth. Both girls gulped.

"She asked to have a word with you, so of course I said you were at the disco."

Silence.

"You hadn't told your parents you were going,

had you?"

"No," whispered Sumitha.

"And now your parents are very put out with me," said Mrs. Turnbull. "Apparently, your father has on more than one occasion expressly forbidden you to go to The Stomping Ground. And now he thinks that I encouraged you to go behind his back. Your father is displeased with me and I, not to put too fine a point on it, am furious with the pair of you. How could you be so deceitful?"

Sumitha looked downcast. "I'm sorry, Mrs. Turnbull," she sniffed. "It's just that—well, Mum and Dad never let me do half the things my friends do. And they were going to the dance, and I was coming here anyway and it seemed . . . "

"It seemed like a good way of doing what you wanted without creating waves," finished Mrs. Turnbull.

"Yes," said Sumitha.

"Well, all I can say is that you have made waves for me. Your mother will probably never trust me again."

"Why did she have to ring?" said Sumitha sullenly. "She's always checking up on me."

"She rang because when they got to the dinner

dance, your mother found your bracelet on the back seat of the car. She thought you would be worrying about having lost it."

"Oh." In fact, Sumitha hadn't even noticed that her bracelet was missing.

Mrs. Turnbull turned to Laura. "I blame you just as much, Laura," she said. "You knew what was going on."

"It's not my fault," said Laura. "I can't tell my friends what to do." And if I could I'd tell her to lay off Jon or else, she thought to herself.

"Mrs. Turnbull," said Sumitha. "I—er—I—well, I mean, we are home and everything went fine and I'm okay—and well, couldn't you tell my mum and dad that discos aren't that bad? They seem to think that something terrible is going to happen to me if I go—but perhaps if you . . . I mean, you let Laura go."

"Sumitha, I can't interfere between you and your parents. You must see—it wouldn't be fair. They have rules and what they tell you to do is up to them." She looked at Sumitha's woebegone face. "But yes, all right, if the opportunity presents itself, I will try and reassure them about the place. It's not so bad."

"Oh, thanks, Mrs. Turnbull, I'd really appreciate that," said Sumitha.

"You're so lucky, Laura, having a mum who understands," Sumitha said to Laura later while they were getting ready for bed.

And just for a fleeting moment, Laura felt rather proud. Then she had a mental picture of Sumitha dancing with Jon.

"I'm going to have a shower," she snapped, and stomped to the bathroom. Sumitha sat on the bed and thought of Jon.

"Good evening, was it, Chelsea?" Ginny yawned as she yanked a piece of paper out of her printer and switched off her computer.

"Yes, it was great and Mum . . . " began Chelsea.

"Oh good, that's nice. Well, I'm for my bed—just done fifteen hundred words on How to Put the Sparkle Back in Your Marriage, and on Monday I'm interviewing a beekeeper in Hackleton in the morning and a man who breeds piranha fish in the afternoon. No peace for the wicked."

"That's nice. Mum, there was this boy . . . "

"Oh, boys is it? Going to write a poem about him, are you?"

"Pardon?"

"I found your little literary outpouring when I

was defrosting the fridge earlier," said Ginny. "It seems you'd rather have a mother who dressed like Claire Farrant than one who tries to keep abreast of trends."

Chelsea gulped. "No, Mum, of course I wouldn't," she said. "I mean, most of the time you look great." (Well, some of the time, she thought to herself.) "It's just that—well, sometimes it would be nice if you looked more mumlike. Not so sort of noticeable," she added.

"Oh well, that's me, I'm afraid. Take me or leave me, as they say. Oh, did I tell you, I'm going to do a four page supplement on Ghosts of Leehampton. Haunted houses, headless highwaymen, that sort of stuff. Good, eh?"

Chelsea gave up. She couldn't compete with the features pages of the *Echo*. It was pointless trying. Her mother was more interested in phantoms and piranhas than her own daughter. And tomorrow Rob would be round and Chelsea really wanted him to like her. But she was scared too. She'd never had a proper boyfriend and she did so want to make a good impression. She didn't want to come on too strong but on the other hand, she wanted him to know she liked him. Her mum spent her life telling

other people how to handle their relationships, so why couldn't she take the time to help her own daughter?

There was one other niggling little worry on Chelsea's mind. Rob had seemed pretty impressed by Mum's job. If he came round and Mum started gushing and exclaiming and thrusting her bosoms around, she would frighten Rob away. And there was no way Chelsea wanted that to happen.

"So you went to the disco, I see." Jon's father was at the front door when Rob's dad dropped him off. "I trust you will do some revision tomorrow—mock exams are not that far off."

"Dad, I've already done heaps," sighed Jon. "And anyway, the subject I like best you can't revise for. I'm sick of swotting up about the Civil War and continental shelves and French verbs. I hate all that stuff. I . . . "

"Ah, but 'that stuff' as you call it is just what you need on your cv for university," began his father. "I've heard that they set great store . . . "

"I AM NOT GOING TO UNIVERSITY!" shouted Jon.

"Oh don't let's start all that again, son," said his

father. "With a brain like yours, where else would you go?"

"To art college, actually," said Jon. I've done it, he thought. I've said it.

His father stared at him. He opened his mouth but nothing happened.

"I want to study art and design, Dad," said Jon. "I'm good at it, I enjoy it and I know I can make a living from it. And the best place to learn more is at art college."

"Art college? ART COLLEGE?" Jon's father blustered. Jon might as well have announced that he wanted to retire to a cardboard box under Waterloo Bridge.

"Yes—I want to be a political cartoonist," said Jon. That's done it, he thought.

A spluttering noise came out of his father's throat. His cheeks took on a livid purple hue.

"I've never heard such . . . it's preposterous . . . what are you thinking of, lad?"

"My future," said Jon. And went to bed.

27 Confessions in the Night

Sumitha was puzzled. Laura was in a very strange mood. She had come back from the shower, jumped into bed, muttered "good night," and turned off the light.

Normally when Sumitha stayed over, they lay awake talking about everything—clothes, school, boys, discos, the top ten, boys, ambitions, boys . . .

"It was good tonight, wasn't it?" ventured Sumitha.

Silence.

"Well, I thought it was really great," continued Sumitha.

The duvet was flung off Laura's bed and she sat up. "Oh yes, well you would think it was great, wouldn't you?" Laura snapped.

Sumitha was taken aback. "What do you mean?" she asked.

"Oh don't come the little miss innocent with me—you know jolly well what I mean!" shouted Laura. And then to Sumitha's horror, she burst into tears.

Sumitha jumped out of her bed and went to sit by Laura. "Hey, Laura—what's wrong? What's the matter?" she asked.

"You're what's wrong, if you must know! You spent nearly all evening with Jon and it's not fair!" sobbed Laura. "He's my friend, not yours. One minute you say your dad doesn't let you have boyfriends and the next you are dashing around stealing everyone else's!"

Sumitha stared at her. "But I didn't know he was your boyfriend—honest I didn't," said Sumitha. "You never said—how long have you been going out?"

Laura sniffed. "Well, we aren't going out exactly," she said.

"So what's the score?" asked Sumitha. She needed to know just where she stood—she really liked Jon, and he hadn't seemed that interested in Laura. Come to think of it, Sumitha couldn't recall having

seen them together at all. Was this another case of Laura's imagination running riot?

Laura related the saga of the bike smash and Jon's legs and his crooked smile and how she really wanted him to like her.

"And now, thanks to you, my entire life is in ruins," cried Laura.

Sumitha sighed. "Oh come on, Laura, spare me the dramatics," she said. "First you tell me that Jon is your boyfriend—then it turns out you've known him for one day. Anyway, if he'd wanted to dance with you, he only had to ask, didn't he? Or didn't that occur to you?"

Laura said nothing.

"And anyway, I didn't ask him to dance. He just grabbed me and said, 'Let's dance,' and then we got talking about parents and life and what we wanted to do and stuff. He danced with Chelsea, too—and Jemma and that girl Melanie from Year Ten," she added, not wishing to carry the full force of Laura's wrath single handed.

"So why didn't he dance with me, then?" asked Laura, wiping her eyes on the corner of her duvet. "Because you wouldn't let him, probably."

"Oh don't be so melodramatic—why would I do

that?" argued Sumitha. "Were you nice to him this morning?"

"Course I was," said Laura. "Well, eventually. We had a few words at first about idiots who couldn't apply their brakes and stuff but then he was really nice. And tonight he just ignored me."

"Perhaps," said Sumitha, thinking quickly, "perhaps he's so madly in love with you that he can't bring himself to speak to you—that happened in *Beverly Hills 90210* once," she added, to give authenticity to her idea.

"Really?" said Laura, perking up.

"Oh yes," said Sumitha, "it's a known fact that boys get so overcome by their emotions because they are less able to cope with things than girls are—my *Growing Up* book said—and so they pretend to be all macho and offhand and stuff when really they are burning with passion."

Laura looked considerably more cheerful.

"Maybe I'll get to see him again when I go to Jemma's," she said. "Anyway, you promise to leave him alone in future, don't you?"

Sumitha sighed. She liked Jon, she really did. And she thought he liked her—in fact, she didn't think he liked Laura as much as Laura wanted to

believe. Sumitha had never had a proper boyfriend and probably never would if her father had anything to do with it. But she liked Laura, too. She said nothing.

"Sumitha—you promise, don't you? Cross your heart and hope to die?"

"I can't," said Sumitha, honestly. "Why should I? If he likes you, he'll pluck up the courage to tell you soon enough. And if he likes me more, I can't help it, can I?"

"You're evil!" shouted Laura. "You're just like that awful Betsy—you're a man stealer; you go around wrecking other people's lives. I hate you!" And with that she pulled the duvet over her head, hurled herself against the wall and refused to say another word.

Sumitha felt awful. She hated making promises she couldn't keep, and she knew that if Jon wanted to be her friend she wouldn't say no. She also knew that Laura was very upset about her dad moving out and seemed to be getting in a state about everything these days. Perhaps she'd be friends again in the morning. Meanwhile, she would just go to sleep and dream of Jon.

Laura lay awake, hating Sumitha, hating the

world, and most of all hating herself. How could Jon like her, with her ghastly ginger hair and freckles when he could have Sumitha, with her pixie face and gorgeous black eyes? Perhaps, she thought, she could win him over with her intellect. But somehow she doubted it. Boys, she had already discovered, rank intellect fairly low on the agenda.

She began working out the plot for her next novel about a girl whose lover was stolen away by an evil temptress. She had just got to the bit where the girl wreaked revenge with a poisoned pizza when she fell asleep.

28
The Morning After the Night Before

Dawn broke grey, overcast, and threatening in Leehampton, and in at least three households, the mood mirrored the weather. Laura and Sumitha sat silently at the breakfast table, which was unusual, because normally when Sumitha stayed over, Mrs. Turnbull couldn't hear herself think for chattering and giggling. This morning, they had the appearance of two doomed souls. She assumed Sumitha was worrying about her forthcoming meeting with her irate father, and Laura was suffering from guilt pangs about her behaviour. Not that Mrs. Turnbull spent much time worrying about it—she was still bothered about her conversation with Peter. Had he implied that it was she who was making Laura miserable? Doubtless Laura would have a field day when she saw her father next weekend, recounting her mother's imagined exploits with Melvyn. Compared with motherhood, splitting the atom must have been a doddle, she thought.

On Billing Hill, all was not sweetness and light. At number 47, Mr. and Mrs. Joseph were seated at the breakfast bar; Jon was still asleep. Mrs. Joseph was feeling a little bleary-eyed; her irate husband had crashed into the bedroom the previous evening and spent the next hour holding forth about the ingratitude of his son, and how he had no doubt it was his mother who had put this ridiculous idea into his head, and did she honestly think he had spent the last fifteen years working all the hours God made to educate his son, just to see him throw it all down the drain?

"Maybe," his sleepy wife had ventured to suggest, "Jon just doesn't share your ambition."

"And what would you know about ambition?" jeered Mr Joseph, thumping his pillow in annoyance. "You've never had any—been quite happy to make your posies and teach people how to fiddle around with flowers. Well, that's you. I had to do things the hard way—night school, taking any job that came my way, pulling myself up the executive

ladder by my shoelaces. And I made it, didn't I?"

"Yes, dear, you've done wonderfully well," murmured Mrs. Joseph, wishing he would shut up long enough for her to get to sleep.

Her husband grunted. "But it's going to be different for Jon. Jon is going to hit the big time. And he won't do it going to some third-rate art college."

"So let him go to a first-rate one, then," retorted his wife, to her own utter amazement. "What's the point of keep trying to get him to do something that's going to make him miserable? Doesn't happiness count for something?"

Her husband had looked at her witheringly. "Happiness, Anona, does not pay the bills."

"And there's no point being miserable in comfort, either," snapped his wife. "I should know—you say I never had any ambition, but what chance did I have to do what I really wanted? None. And why? Because I was doing my best to support you while you studied and worked. I didn't begrudge it, I admired you and I was pleased to see you happy. But doing that sort of thing won't make Jon happy, and the sooner you realise it, the better."

Henry Joseph had lain awake for a long time that night. First, the shock of his son's ridiculous choice

of career had bowled him over, and then his wife, normally so manageable, had flown off the handle and virtually accused him of holding her back. Stuff and nonsense. It was her age, no doubt about it. Women turned funny after forty, he knew that. But he still couldn't get to sleep.

And now Henry was taking his anger out on an innocent piece of toast, slamming on the butter with total disregard to hardening arteries and high cholesterol. His wife, meanwhile, was calmly reading *Floral Arts* magazine and wondering whether she could make a Japanese willow arrangement for Mrs. Farrant next door.

"Anyway," grunted Henry, "what would you have done, if you had had a choice?"

His wife raised her eyes from the page in surprise. "Oh, interior design, dear. And actually, it's not too late. I'm thinking of becoming a mature student."

For only the second time in his life, Henry Joseph was lost for words.

Next door at Number 49, Mr. Farrant was enjoying a leisurely Sunday breakfast and revelling in the fact that today he did not have to dash to the hospital to remove a paper clip from some five-year-

old's left ear, or yank out a couple of dozen tonsils before lunch. He was hunched over a bowl of muesli, which his wife assured him was frightfully nutritious (though he would have preferred sausages and bacon), reflecting on his first few weeks at Leehampton General and flicking through the pages of *The Lancet*.

Not that it was a very quiet breakfast. The twins were having a competition to see who could flick the milk from their cereal bowls the furthest and Sam was sitting under the table being a Monster From Outer Space which involved chewing his father's left ankle. Jemma was gazing into her mug of tea with the expression of awaiting the firing squad.

"Come on Jemma, eat up now," encouraged her mother.

"Oh, leave me alone!" muttered Jemma.

"Jemma!" admonished her father. "Don't speak to your mother like that! What has got into you?"

"I'm fed up with being treated like a kid of nine," said Jemma.

"Well, maybe when your manners are those of an adult you will be treated as such," interrupted her mother.

Jemma burst into tears and rushed out of the room.

"What brought all that on?" asked Mr. Farrant.

And his wife related the saga of the clothes and the makeup and the disco and waited for her husband to reassure her that she was perfectly right and that she was the best judge of what was right for the children.

"Jemma does have a point, dear," he said instead. "She is almost fourteen and frankly, she usually looks about eleven. And it has to be said, you do tend to go on a bit, don't you?"

His wife stared at him.

"Look," he said, "I know you worry about her, but the one thing you cannot control is the passage of time. She's growing up and there isn't a thing you can do to stop that."

"But she's just a little girl," began his wife.

Mr. Farrant, who was used to keeping calm in crises, when people bled on to the floor of the operating theatre, or a trainee nurse dropped a scalpel onto his toe, decided that it was Sunday and who cared? He thumped his fist on the table.

"No, Claire—she is not a little girl. Not anymore. She is rapidly turning into a young woman—

or as rapidly as you will let her. And let me tell you something else. If you don't acknowledge that fact pretty fast, you will lose her. And you don't want that, do you?"

Claire Farrant poured herself another mug of tea and started doing some serious thinking.

Two hours later, Laura's mum was entertaining. Or rather, pacifying. Either side of her kitchen table sat Rajiv and Chitrita Banerji, the former looking very severe and erect, the latter rather scared and shrunken. They had come to collect their daughter, who had disappeared rather smartly the moment their car was heard pulling up outside.

"I really had no idea that you had told Sumitha she was not to go to The Stomping Ground," repeated Ruth, pouring proper coffee from her cafetière (she thought the Banerjis in their present mood warranted the filter stuff and not the instant). "Naturally, had I known, I would have kept Laura home too. But no harm's been done," she added.

"I am sure, Mrs. Turnbull, that you meant no harm," said Chitrita, nibbling on a piece of supermarket flapjack that Ruth was trying to pretend was homemade.

"I am not in favour of such places," said Rajiv. He was dressed in a dark suit and blue pin-striped shirt and looked more as if he was ready for a board meeting than a relaxing Sunday, thought Ruth. She wondered whether he ever let his hair down.

"Sumitha knew that; she had no right to deceive you. The fault lies with her," Mr. Banerji continued. "But I am surprised you did not think to consult my wife and I about the decision."

Ruth gulped. She wondered whether Mr. Banerji was as fierce as this with all the patients he X-rayed. "I agree. That was entirely my fault. When Sumitha said that you . . . anyway, I see it this way," began Ruth, taking her life into her hands. "These days our children have to learn to live in the world as it is, not as we would prefer it to be. I feel that the occasional evening like this—and they are very well supervised, I made sure of that—gives them a taste of freedom without too great a risk. And of course, a girl as well brought-up as Sumitha . . . "

"Exactly. She is indeed a well brought-up girl—and not accustomed to such places," emphasised Mr. Banerji. But Ruth noticed that his expression had mellowed a little at praise of his daughter.

"I think she didn't want to upset you—and yet

she wanted to go with all her friends. Such a charming girl is bound to be popular—Laura tells me that she is an amazing dancer," said Mrs. Turnbull, grovelling like crazy. "You must be proud of her."

Ten minutes later, after a rundown of Sumitha's prowess at drama and dance, her ability to make a wonderful Khashir Rezala, and her great likeness to the paternal grandmother in Calcutta, Rajiv stood up.

"You believe I am hard in forbidding my daughter to attend. Perhaps so," he said, inclining his head.

Sumitha, who was listening at the door with Laura, gave her the thumbs up. "Your mum is absolutely brilliant," she whispered. "She's a miracle worker."

Laura was about to smile when she remembered she had not forgiven Sumitha.

"But," Mr. Banerji continued, "I act in the interests of my daughter's reputation. I would not want her turning out like most English girls. Many of them have no self-respect. We have standards, you see."

"And so, Mr. Banerji, do most English families," said Ruth quietly.

"Of course they do, of course they do," interrupted the hitherto-acquiescent Chitrita. "We are all parents trying to do our best, are we not? And often, I fear, getting it wrong. Raising children, it is not an easy task. My daughter, she thinks I am prehistoric. But then, that is life, I suppose—being derided by one's offspring." She smiled and turned to pick up her handbag. "We must meet again for a talk, we two." She winked at Ruth. "We are going now, Rajiv. Come, Sumitha," she called. "Come, Rajiv."

And to everyone's surprise, not least his own, Rajiv did as he was told.

In Thorburn Crescent, Chelsea was reapplying her eyeshadow for the third time since breakfast when the doorbell rang.

"Get the door, Chelsea, can you?" Ginny called from the kitchen.

But Chelsea was already there.

"Hi, you said it'd be okay to call round." Rob stood on the doorstep looking incredibly edible in a pair of maroon cycling shorts. He grinned and Chelsea's intestines did a double back flip with pike.

"Sure—come in," Chelsea said, wondering if her kneecaps would continue to hold her up. She led Rob into the kitchen. "Mum, this is Rob."

"Hello, Rob—coffee?" Ginny brandished the cafetière.

"Please." Rob flicked back a quiff of sandy hair and grinned again.

"It was good last night, wasn't it?" said Chelsea, wishing she could think of something more sparkling to say. Her heart was behaving in a highly undisciplined manner.

"Yeah, I had a really good time," said Rob and turned to Ginny. "Mrs. Gee, I've read loads of your stuff in the *Echo*—my mum thinks you're tremendous."

"Well, thank you, Rob," said Ginny, giving him one of her most dazzling smiles. "And please, do call me Ginny."

Chelsea cringed.

"Actually, I want to be a journalist," said Rob, "and I was just wondering . . . "

"Do you want to come upstairs and listen to my new Crackdown CD?" said Chelsea in desperation, knowing precisely where this conversation would lead.

Rob ignored her. "I was wondering whether you could give me some tips—you know, about subjects to take and how to get work experience, that sort of thing."

"Well, I'd be happy to," said Ginny. "Of course, that's if you really think that silly old me..." Chelsea fought down a desire to vomit.

"Oh, anything you can tell me will be such a help," said Rob.

Ginny fluttered her (well, Superdrug's) eyelashes. "Well, in my experience, what you need to do is..."

Ten minutes later Ginny said, "Chelsea, make us some more coffee, love. Now, Rob, take a look at this piece I did on latchkey kids..."

Chelsea's stomach was all knotted up. She thought she might cry.

Fifteen minutes later, Ginny said, "Chelsea, I think there's some shortbread in the green tin—be a love."

Silently Chelsea hoped her mother might choke on it.

Twenty minutes later, Chelsea grabbed the opportunity of her mother leaving the room to find her copy of *The Writers' Handbook* to say, "Rob, do you want to come up and see…"

"Oh sorry, no, I'd better be going soon. My mum will blow a fuse if I am late for lunch. Thanks a million, Mrs. . . . Ginny," he said, as Ginny swept back into the room. "I'll bring some of my stuff round some time and perhaps you can tell me what you think."

"Be happy to, Rob. And have a go at that Young Writer's Competition. Nice to have met you. Ciao!"

"Bye, Rob," said Chelsea.

"Cheers, Chelsea, see you around," said Rob. But he didn't look round.

"Well thank you very much, Mum," said Chelsea and flounced upstairs. She threw herself on the bed and burst into tears.

"I hate her, Aardvark," she sobbed. "Not content with showing off in front of the world, now she's stealing my boyfriend. I hate her!"

29 Friendships Under Strain

It had been a pretty horrid week. Not only would Laura not speak to Sumitha, but she did her best to stop Chelsea and Jemma doing so as well.

"But why?" asked Chelsea, whose logical and scientific mind always demanded reasons for agreeing to do anything. "She hasn't done anything to me."

"Oh great, some friend you turned out to be!" snapped Laura. "She just tried to take Jon away from me, that's all!"

"But Jon was never with you!" said Chelsea. "How can you have something taken away when you never had it in the first place?"

Laura sniffed. She didn't want to admit to herself that Chelsea had a point.

"Anyway, he's got spots," said Chelsea. Rob didn't have any spots. Rob was wonderful. But thanks to her mother, she'd probably never get the chance to be alone with him for a single second.

Laura went off in a huff and cornered Jemma.

"You're my friend, aren't you?" she demanded.

"Of course," said Jemma.

"So you won't have anything to do with Sumitha, will you?" she asked.

Jemma gulped. She wanted to be friends with everyone. And besides, she had nothing against Sumitha. In fact, she had got on with her very well at the disco. They both knew what it was to have difficult parents.

"Well, I mean, I—well, she's really nice," she said.

"Nice? Nice? You call wrecking relationships nice? How would you feel if she stole your boyfriend? Not that you are likely to ever find out—I don't suppose Mummy will ever let you off the leading reins long enough to get one!"

And she stormed off, leaving Jemma feeling terrible. As if things weren't bad enough as it was: her mother was acting all injured and silent, even though Jemma had said sorry a dozen times; her newfound friends were at loggerheads; Laura, who had started out being so nice to her, thought she was a baby like all the others; and Gran still hadn't replied to her letter.

Sumitha felt awful too. If she really thought that Jon was Laura's boyfriend, she wouldn't have dreamt of muscling in. But he wasn't—she knew that. Anyway, it was pointless worrying about it. He went to a different school, was a year older—she'd probably never see him again. Except. Except that Dad, after much muttering behind closed doors with her mother, had announced that providing all his rules were adhered to, she could go to The Stomping Ground once a month. He had actually smiled when he said it. And if Jon went there regularly, she just might see him again. But somehow, with the argument with Laura still hanging over her head, she didn't feel as good about it as she should.

Chelsea's week went from bad to worse. On Tuesday night, Rob called round—and spent forty-five minutes closeted round the table with her mother, discussing his entry for the Young Writer of the Year competition. On Thursday morning, he called on the way to school but only to show her mum the finished article.

So by Thursday morning, which was double

English, which Chelsea hated, followed by double science which Laura loathed and current affairs which none of them liked, the mood was not good. Jemma and Chelsea were fed up with mothers, Sumitha was fed up with Laura and Laura was resolved to hate the Bestial Betsy and Sumitha in equal amounts for the rest of her life. And then, suddenly and most surprisingly, things started looking up.

Meanwhile Jon, the unwitting cause of so much tension, had been having a rather better time. He'd felt more at ease since coming clean with his father—even if he had been furious. And Parents' Evening was quite soon, he was sure his teachers would be complimentary about his art. That is, if his blustering father let them get a word in edgeways.

30
Confidences Over Coffee

That Thursday morning, while the girls were brooding on the injustices of life, their mothers were drinking coffee in Mrs. Farrant's sitting room and attempting to make some sort of sense of the world they lived in.

Jemma's mum had thought the coffee session would give her the chance to get to know the other mothers a bit better and make her peace with Mrs. Turnbull. She had been so busy worrying about her husband's new job, and Jemma's new school, and whether Samuel was going down with the mumps, that she had only just realised how much she was missing all her old friends. And she knew she had been rather snappy when she dropped the girls off after the disco, and wanted to patch things up.

Ruth was a bit wary of facing everyone after

Laura had taken to the airwaves, but she knew she'd have to do it some time. And Ginny was probably right maybe no one had heard it. Mrs. Banerji was delighted at the prospect of a chat away from the somewhat domineering presence of her husband and Ginny, who when Jemma's mother had phoned, had been throwing dictionaries around her study, partly because she was suffering from writers' block—and partly because Barry had been unusually pointed about her new floral leggings, was glad of an excuse to forget earning a living for a couple of hours. And Mrs. Joseph, thought that meeting a few new people would be much more stimulating than worrying about family relationships.

The conversation inevitably came round to the kids.

"I've decided that I am going to buy Jemma some new clothes on Saturday," announced Mrs. Farrant. "Apparently she says I am trying to keep her looking like a baby," she explained. "And I suppose, beside your girls, she does look a bit young for her age."

The others made the sort of noncommittal murmurs that meant they totally agreed but thought it more polite not to say so.

"I must say, I am a bit worried about what she'll choose—she seems to think of nothing but clothes these days and she's taken to reading these teenage magazines."

"Oh, don't worry about it, it's perfectly natural," said Ginny airily, thinking that Claire could do with spending a few minutes considering the same topic. Actually, that might make quite a nifty little column for next week's slot. Mother vs. Daughter Fashion Stakes. There—she'd broken the writer's block already. "I remember when Geneva was twelve, she turned up in black fishnet tights and a satin over shirt. She looked like a reject from the Follies Bergère."

"Surely you didn't let her go round like that?" gasped Claire.

"Oh yes," said Ginny. "After four neighbours had fallen over in hysterics, she got the message. It would have taken me hours of in-house fighting."

"How sensible," sighed Chitrita. "I fear I am not a very good mother. You see, Rajiv is a stubborn man. He adores Sumitha but he is very strict. And me, I hate to cause an argument. I fear Sumitha suffers for her mother's weakness."

They all murmured sympathetically, secretly feeling relieved that someone else was failing to match up to the psychologists' idea of Supermum.

"You and me both," said Mrs. Joseph suddenly. "For years I've watched my husband mapping out Jon's life for him, and I've just gone along with it. Henry had to struggle to get to where he is today, you see, and I think in a way he wants to relive his life through Jon. He seems set on Jon going to university, but Jon wants to go to art college. Henry really blew his top," she said wryly.

Chitrita sighed. "That's like my Rajiv. Sumitha wants to have her hair cut shorter. In India this is not customary but I say to Rajiv, we are not in India now. But he won't budge. So what can I do?"

"Well," said Anona Joseph decisively, "I for one am changing. I'm going to back Jon all the way. Although I'm scared stiff of what Henry will say. And what's more I'm going back to college myself."

She told them her plans to train to be an interior designer, and set up her own consultancy one day. They were very impressed. Then Mrs. Turnbull told them how she was going for yet another interview next week.

"It's for a primary school secretary," she said.

"Maybe they won't need me to be a computer whiz-kid!"

"Well, good for you," said Ginny. "I'll keep my fingers crossed."

"Soon you'll be the only one being a good Earth Mother at home," remarked Ginny to Mrs. Farrant, as she topped up her coffee.

"Yes," sighed Claire. "Actually, I used to love all the homemaking bit but sometimes these days, I wish I could get out more . . ."

"Well, I could always use help with my English as a Second Language classes," remarked Mrs. Banerji. "There are never enough helpers for the students to practice their English on. Come while the children are at playgroup," said Mrs. Banerji. "You'd enjoy it."

I think I might, thought Mrs. Farrant. At least it would be something else to think about rather than this business with Jemma.

"I suppose," she said, turning to Ginny, who was on to her third piece of carrot cake, "that you don't have problems with Chelsea, what with you being an expert on relationships and things?"

Ginny grimaced. "Don't you believe it. It's much easier telling other people how to live their lives

than managing to sort your own out. Right now, Chelsea is not impressed with me."

"But doesn't that worry you?" said Jemma's mother. "I mean, don't you get in a state when they have these outbursts and want to do outrageous things?"

"Of course I do," said Ginny, "but worrying doesn't stop them growing up and at the end of the day, they have to make a few mistakes of their own."

She paused. "Warwick's off to Indonesia tomorrow and I'm worried sick—but what can I do? He's an adult, he likes trees more than people, and he's determined to go. I've told him to phone," she added, "but Warwick is not very good at remembering instructions. And Chelsea thinks I should be home all the time attending to her needs."

"Well, if it's any consolation," said Ruth, "Laura thinks you are Mother of the Year—how many times has she said to me, 'Oh Mum, why can't you be like Chelsea's mother?' Apparently you are with it, and I am without it; you are of the nineties and I am antediluvian; you know the meaning of life, I know nothing . . . shall I go on?"

"I suppose," said Mrs. Farrant, topping up everyone's coffee, "that the next thing we shall have to contend with is boyfriends. Now that really does

worry me."

Everything seems to worry you, thought Ginny, but just smiled.

"Oh, it's starting already," said Mrs. Turnbull. "Last term Laura had a crush on Duncan Nisbet, but that seems to have petered out. I was wondering if she'd found someone else."

"Chelsea met this lad called Rob at the disco—in Year Ten at school apparently," said Ginny.

"Oh yes, he's a great friend of Jon's," said Mrs. Joseph. "They were at primary school together."

"Nice lad, keeps phoning me for tips on becoming a journalist. One likes to help them if one can," Ginny added.

"So you're stealing your daughter's boyfriends now, are you?" teased Ruth.

"Oh, Chelsea doesn't think of him as a boyfriend . . . well, I don't think she does. I mean, she never said. And he's never seemed to take much notice of . . . I never thought. He just said they'd met at The Stomping Ground and he'd discovered that I was Chelsea's mum and . . . oh, goodness, you don't think that Chelsea's feeling peeved because all he wants to do is talk about writing and all she wants is his attention all to herself?"

No one said a word.

Ginny started thinking.

"Sumitha has no boyfriends," said Chitrita. "Her father would not permit it."

As if that will make any difference, thought the other mothers simultaneously.

"Well, she seemed quite fond of your Jon . . . " began Claire.

"Oh, goodness, is that the time?" said Ruth hastily. "I must be going."

"Jon?" said Chitrita, puzzled.

"Yes, Anona's boy. She said he was a friend . . . " said Claire doubtfully, as Mrs. Joseph and Mrs. Banerji looked at one another in surprise.

A virtual reality shot of Sumitha's father when he discovered his daughter had consorted with a boy swam before Ruth's eyes. Drastic circumstances called for drastic action.

"Oh, no, I'm so sorry, Claire!" Ruth cried as the mug of coffee landed in her hostess's lap.

In the ensuing dash for cold water and cloths and tissues and kitchen roll, the subject of discos was quite forgotten.

Mrs. Banerji had put two and two together and made four. She wasn't worried—it had to happen some time and Sumitha was a sensible girl—but she knew Rajiv would disapprove strongly. She decided to forget what she had heard.

Claire Farrant was clucking around with a damp cloth.

Well, thought Ruth as she looked guiltily at Claire's stained tweed, we didn't want a scene, did we?

On the Up

When Jemma got in from school on Thursday, her mother sat her down and said, “So what sort of clothes would you really like to wear? Not,” she added hastily, “that you will necessarily get them.”

Jemma gulped. “Well,” she said, “a mini-kilt would be great.” She said the word “mini” very softly and emphasised the “kilt” bit. “And perhaps some patent clogs. Or a satin shirt, a forties-style jacket, a crushed velvet waistcoat . . . ”

Her mother sighed. “Oh, dear, I don’t know—but I suppose you are nearly fourteen.”

“Yes I am,” said Jemma. “That’s what I’ve been trying to tell you all this time.”

“Okay, okay,” said her mother, determined to avoid another row. “I’ll tell you what. You can buy some new clothes. We’ll go out next Saturday and pop into Tammy Girl and . . . ”

"MUM!"

"Sorry, sorry. Streetwise, Miss Dynamite, wherever . . . "

"That would be great, Mum, it really would," said Jemma. "But could I take Laura or Sumitha or someone and go on my own? I mean, it's not really on to have your mum tagging along in town."

"Oh I see. And are your friends going to be footing the bill for this spending extravaganza?"

"No, but . . . "

Her mum sighed. Count to ten, she told herself. "All right. You go with the girls, choose your clothes and I'll meet you later on to write the cheque."

Jemma leapt up and hugged her mum. "Thanks, Mum—I'll phone the others."

"But you'll see them tomorrow," called her mother.

But Jemma was already dialling.

32
Shop Till You Drop

Sumitha had been delighted when Jemma had phoned to ask her about shopping on Saturday. She had just decided to take the plunge and have her hair cut while her father was in a better mood. Jemma had asked whether this wasn't pushing her luck a bit, but Sumitha knew that it was something she simply had to do. But it would help to have Jemma there for moral support.

The next day at school Jemma asked Chelsea and Laura to go along too. Secretly she wanted someone with her who wasn't as slim as a reed and stunningly beautiful and she thought Laura fitted the bill. But Laura pouted and said she would go only if Sumitha didn't, and Jemma did something very unusual for her. She lost her temper.

"Oh pull yourself together, Laura, and stop whining!" she shouted. "All this fuss over a boy who probably hasn't given either of you another thought since Saturday. What matters more—friends you've got, or one boy who might speak to you again if he's nothing better to do?"

Laura looked sheepish. Truth to tell, she was getting tired of playing the wounded party.

"Golly, Jemma, I didn't know you had it in you," said Chelsea admiringly, when Laura and Sumitha had grudgingly agreed not to mention Jon again and to be friends.

So they went to town and Jemma chose a knee grazer skirt, a mini-shift in luminous pink, and two cropped tops. Her only problem was devising a way to convince her mother that these were essential items in the wardrobe of any self-respecting fourteen-year-old.

"What you need," Chelsea suggested, "is a strategy. Show her something outrageous first—those gold PVC dungarees over there. Then, when she throws a total whoopsie . . . "

"Which she will," interjected Jemma.

"When she throws a total whoopsie," continued Chelsea, "you say—'Okay, mum, how about these?' and show her the ones you really want. Good, eh?"

"Brilliant," said Jemma.

Then it was Sumitha's turn. She had bought three pairs of dangly earrings and was impatient to get her hair cut so that she could show them off. The girls marched into Fringe Affairs and watched as Sumitha's jet-black hair fell in a growing pile to the floor.

An hour later, Sumitha emerged with a neat bob and a very cold neck. And burst into tears.

"I hate it!" she wept.

"It looks great," said Chelsea.

"It really suits you," agreed Laura, thinking that Jon wouldn't fancy her half so much without all that gorgeous long hair.

"Wish my hair hung like that," added Jemma.

It had taken two doughnuts and a mug of hot chocolate to pacify Sumitha and it wasn't until she had put on one of her pairs of new earrings and received an admiring glance from a rather dishy boy at the opposite table that she calmed down.

"Now all I have to do is face the music at home," she sighed, as she left for the bus stop.

When Mrs. Farrant arrived at Togs 'n' Clogs at the appointed time, having told herself over and over again to be calm, laid back and adult, Jemma showed her the gold dungarees.

"YOU CANNOT, YOU WILL NOT, GO AROUND IN THOSE!" screeched Mrs. Farrant, causing the manager of Togs 'n' Clogs to drop her polystyrene cup of coffee in alarm.

"Okay, okay, Mum, whatever you say," said Jemma. "Do you prefer these?"

She held up the skirt, the pink shift and one of the tops.

"The skirt's incredibly short, the dress is very bright—oh, go on then. Take them. Anything's better than those awful plastic things."

"Thanks, Mum, you're a star." Jemma grinned as her mother drew out her cheque book. She gave the thumbs-up to the others.

"Children," sighed Mrs. Farrant to the shop assistant who was applying great concentration to chewing on some gum. "Bless them, they do grow up so fast don't they? It only seems the other day…"

"Mum, shut up!" muttered Jemma.

The assistant chewed on, folding the clothes into a carrier bag with all the speed of a tortoise on tranquillisers.

"Er, just a moment," said Jemma's mother. "Is that hem coming down?"

"What?"

"I said, is that hem coming down?" She pointed to a couple of stray threads.

"Oh, it's just where it was finished off," said the assistant.

"Well, it obviously isn't finished off, is it? It's not good enough, it is simply not good enough." Jemma's mum was in full flood. "I told my daughter not to shop in cheap places like this but she wouldn't listen. Now, can you find me one that isn't falling apart—or does all your stock disintegrate on touch?"

The assistant raised her plucked eyebrows heavenwards, had another quick chew on her gum, and strolled off. Jemma cringed. Laura and Chelsea were staring openmouthed.

"Oh Mum, don't make a scene," said Jemma, wrapping her left leg round her right one, which she always did when she was mortified. "It's only a tiny bit of hem hanging down—I'll sew it up."

"And look at this." Mrs. Farrant picked up the shirt. "There's a button missing."

"There's a spare inside—I can put that on, Mum. Just pay and don't make a fuss."

"I am not making a fuss, Jemma, I am making a

point. I'm not about to pay good money for a garment only to have it fall to pieces the first instant you put it on."

"It's not falling to pieces—it's . . ."

"ENOUGH!"

The assistant ambled back bearing another skirt. "This do you?" she growled.

Mrs. Farrant examined it. "Thank you, that will do nicely," she said. "And now, this button . . . "

The assistant sighed. "Warrabout it?"

"It isn't there, that's what about it. Of course," said Mrs. Farrant, "I could always deal straight with the manager."

The assistant became alert. "Just one moment, Madam, I'll see if we have one out the back."

"MUM!" Jemma's discomfiture was reaching new heights.

The assistant returned. "I'm sorry, Madam, that's the last one. But I could let you have two pounds off the price."

"Right, that'll do nicely," said Claire.

Laura and Chelsea were impressed. "Your mum knows her stuff," whispered Laura.

"There you are girls," said Claire. "You take the two pounds and get drinks while I go and do the rest of my shopping. I'll see you at home, Jemma."

"Thanks, Mum—really, thanks a lot." Jemma was delighted.

"Your mum was brilliant," said Chelsea. "I'd never have dared say anything."

"She was really pretty cool, wasn't she?" Jemma felt quite proud of her mum. It was something of a novel experience. "I think I'll catch her up and buy her some chocolates—you know, to say thanks."

"Shall I or not?" said Chelsea, as she and Laura sat over their French fries and cola later.

"Shall you or not what?" said Laura, who was quietly worrying about her love life.

"Get my nose pierced," said Chelsea.

"You're not serious?" gasped Laura, the enormity of Chelsea's suggestion banishing even romantic thoughts from her mind. "Your mum would go mad. Well, mine would—yours is pretty cool, so I suppose she wouldn't."

"Come to think of it, she would probably write about it in next week's paper," said Chelsea. "'The Day Chelsea Went Punk'—I wouldn't put it past her. Hey, if you do get your nose pierced, what happens when you catch a cold?"

"Yuk," said Laura.

"Well, then, I'll get my ears done."

"They've been done," said Laura.

"Again," said Chelsea. "Come on."

Sumitha crept through the back door. She tiptoed to the stairs. She met her mother coming out of the dining room.

"Sumitha! Your hair!" Chitrita gasped.

Sumitha gulped.

"I'm sorry, Mum, I mean, I thought it would look—and Dad did say he'd let me do more—but if they hadn't done the sides so—and—oh Mum!" And Sumitha burst into tears again.

"Hey, Sumitha," said her mum, giving her a hug, "you are meant to be pleased with it. What's up?"

"I look stupid," gulped Sumitha.

"You look wonderful," declared her mother.

"I do?" asked Sumitha, hopefully.

"You do," said her mother.

"Do you think I look, well, sort of more, you know . . ."

"You look very elegant—quite the young lady."

"Dad'll make a scene," observed Sumitha.

"This is very true," agreed her mother.

33 Heavymetal

"Hi, Chelsea, how did the shopping . . . what in the name of heaven is that?"

"What?" Chelsea gave her mother what she hoped was a cool stare.

"Your ears—you've got half a dozen things in them." Ginny put her hands to her face.

"Three studs and a ring, actually," said Chelsea.

"Well, take them out right now!" said her mother.

"No way," said Chelsea, "I've only just had them done. Why should I?"

"Because the school rules are one stud only; because you look trashy and cheap; because . . ."

"Oh, that's right, suddenly you take notice of how I look. Normally, you can't be bothered to even notice, you're so busy tarting yourself up and flirting with my boyfriend. Well, tough Cheddar because I'm keeping them and . . . "

"Oh no you are not, young lady. Now get them out this instant or I'll . . . "

"You'll WHAT?" screamed Chelsea. "Write about me in the paper? Tell the world how silly Chelsea did something wrong again? These are my ears and I am making a fashion statement. So there." Chelsea was running out of things to say.

Ginny got up and put her arm on Chelsea's shoulder. "Oh Chelsea love, you're far too pretty to need all that metal junk in your ears," she said.

Chelsea looked at her. "That's the first time you've said I'm pretty," said Chelsea. "Am I really?" she added.

Ginny sat down and pulled Chelsea down beside her. "Of course you are, you nincompoop. I'm sorry, love—I suppose I am so used to knowing how gorgeous you are, I forget that you need to know that, too. You're gorgeous, as a matter of fact."

Chelsea looked slightly appeased.

"And what's all this about me flirting?" continued Ginny, recalling the conversation with the others over coffee. "You surely don't mean chatting to Rob?"

"Chatting, you call it?" mumbled Chelsea. "You positively drool over him. It's obscene."

Her mother suppressed the desire to laugh. "I'm sorry love, I didn't think. It's just that he's so keen on the idea of being a writer, and it boosted my ego, someone wanting my opinion on something other than acne and boyfriends! But flirting? That's crazy—he's just a spotty kid!"

"He's not spotty," snapped Chelsea. "Not very."

"You really like Rob, don't you?" said Ginny.

Chelsea shrugged—then nodded.

"Then go for it—and I'll keep out of the way—I promise," said her mother. "But get rid of that metalwork—it's not you, love." She grinned. "I wish I looked like you, I'll tell you that for nothing."

Chelsea smiled a watery smile. "Everyone says you're the smartest mum in my year. You should be—you spend enough time dressing up."

"I suppose I am a bit vain," said Ginny. "When you get middle-age spread and grey hairs sticking through and your chin starts to sag, you have to work flat out to fight Mother Nature. I look in the mirror some mornings and wish I was twenty again. Am I a real drag?"

"Well," said Chelsea "Sometimes you are sort of unmotherlike."

"Tell you what," said Ginny, "let's go out next

weekend after I've done the show. You choose something you like for me to wear, something suitable for mothers," she added, pulling a face, "and I'll treat you to some nice drop earrings for the one hole I am about to let you keep open!"

Chelsea smiled. "Okay," she said, "but you have to promise not to show off in the changing rooms," she added sternly.

"I promise," said Ginny dutifully.

BELLBOROUGH COURT SCHOOL
BELLBOROUGH
NORTHLANDS

Dear Parent,

The Parents' Evening for your son/daughter will be held on Thursday, July 6th at 7.00 p.m. It is sincerely hoped that parents will attend this event, as it provides an opportunity for helpful consultation between school and home and an effective and supportive monitoring of pupil's progress during the year.

Please complete the slip below, on

receipt of which times will be allocated with the appropriate members of staff.
Yours sincerely,

S Ellwood

Stephen Ellwood
Director of Studies

I will/will not be attending the Parents' evening.

I will/will not be accompanied by my son/daughter.

34
Let Me Put It This Way...

Jon was dreading Parents' Evening. A week ago he had told himself that this time he was going to speak out, stand up for himself and what he wanted, and not let his father ride roughshod all over him. That was last week.

Tonight, standing in line waiting with his father to speak to Sweaty (otherwise known as Mr Ellwood, but given his nickname on account of his aversion to antiperspirants) his courage was not quite so much in evidence. He guessed Sweaty would be on Dad's side—teachers always were. He wished Mum had been there as well, but she was lecturing the Women's Institute on The Place of Ferns in the Indoor Garden.

Ever since he had told his father that he wanted to go to art college after GCSEs, relations between them had been strained to say the least. But the odd thing was, his mother had been really laid back about it—positively encouraging, in fact.

She had raised the subject the morning after the disco. "Your father says you want to go to art college when you leave school," she said. "Tell me about it."

So Jon had taken a deep breath and sat down and told her how the only thing that really excited him was putting his ideas down on paper—not in words, but in pictures. He tried to tell her how the idea of spending all day every day drawing fired his imagination. He liked doing cartoons and he dreamed of being a newspaper cartoonist like Mac or Giles. There were lots of other things he thought he'd enjoy, like designing book jackets or even theatrical design. But to find out about it all he needed to go to art college. And to go to art college it would help to have art and design at GCSE and A level, as well as things like ceramics—not stupid history. And Bellborough Court was a very academic school, and not the least bit arty.

Jon snapped his attention back to the present as he heard Sweaty speak.

"Good evening, Mr. Joseph—and Jonathan." Mr. Ellwood waved them to a seat. "Now, let us see—ah, yes. Here's Jonathan's file."

"Now, look here," began Jon's father before the teacher could get a word in edgeways, "my son seems to have his head filled with ideas of art college and such stuff and nonsense. Perhaps you can sort the lad out—I don't seem to be able . . . "

"Splendid idea," said Mr. Ellwood. "As I am sure you realise, Jon is tremendously talented on the art side. Look at this—straight A's all this year. And that design he produced for the cover of the school magazine—such flair. I have often thought it a shame that he wasn't able to spend more time on this side of things."

"But, good Lord, man, Jon's aiming for Cambridge, law, that sort of thing . . . " Jon's father began, his already florid complexion taking on a cerise flush.

"Jon?" Mr. Ellwood turned to Jon with a somewhat surprised expression on his face.

"I don't want to go to university—it's Dad's idea," muttered Jon, his heart pounding. His father was not partial to being contradicted.

Mr. Ellwood sighed inwardly. What on earth possessed this man to imagine that his son was Cambridge material? Jon was struggling on the academic front already and that was just with GCSEs. He took a deep breath.

"Well, to be quite frank with you, Mr. Joseph, Jon is not really an academically inclined lad—and certainly not Cambridge standard, you know," he explained. "Whereas when it comes to art . . . "

"Well, then, it's up to you lot to make sure he becomes Cambridge standard, then, isn't it? What in the blazes do you think I am pouring out all this money for? Flaming art college? If he was going to art college, he might as well be at the local comprehensive."

"I wish I was," Jon heard his voice say, to his extreme surprise.

"JON!" his father expostulated.

By now, three quarters of the room were casting sideways glances at the gesticulating Mr. Joseph. Jon lowered his eyes and prayed that the floor would open and swallow his father up.

"Mr. Joseph," said Mr. Ellwood, mentally counting to ten, "Jon could go a long way in the art world. He shows great promise. As you know, he is studying GCSE art here at Bellborough, but when it comes to A level, he would have more opportunity of achieving his full potential in that field at a school with studios, pottery kilns, all the equipment he needs. And Bellborough is not that sort of school."

"This is preposterous," blustered Henry Joseph. He stood up and turned to Jon, beckoning him to leave. But Jon had already left.

"Perhaps, Mr. Joseph," began Mr. Ellwood, "I could show you something."

35 The Art of Compromise

Jon sat by the bike sheds feeling utterly fed up. When Sweaty had turned up trumps and said how good he was at art, he'd had a sudden burst of hope. But of course, Dad had to go blustering on about what he thought and what he wanted and they hadn't got anywhere.

He knew he wasn't clever—he just about managed, but that was only because he worked flat out. All he wanted to do was design, draw, paint.

He thought about what that girl Sumitha had said: "Go for it—they'll come round in the end." For a few days, he had believed her. Well, she'd been wrong, hadn't she? And for a brief spell, he thought his mother was going to talk Dad round. He wished he had more spunk, a bit like the kid he'd knocked off that bike. I bet she would have stood up for herself, he thought, grinning at the memory of her holding forth in the middle of Billing Hill. I bet when she wants something she just goes out and gets it, he thought.

"We're going, Jon." His father emerged from behind the science block. Jon thought he looked somewhat subdued. They walked to the car in silence.

When they were in the car, his father coughed, looked at Jon, and coughed again. "You didn't say anything about doing a cover for the school magazine," he said.

"There didn't seem much point," said Jon. "After all, magazine covers don't count for Cambridge entrance, so I didn't think you'd be interested."

"Mr. Ellwood showed it to me—it's pretty damn good." Mr. Joseph gave Jon a half-smile.

"Thanks," said Jon.

"He showed me those caricatures of politicians you did, too, and your design for the scenery in the school play. Pretty hot stuff. Look, I . . . well, I think you are wrong. In fact, I think you are mad. But, if you really are set on this art caper, I suppose I shouldn't stop you."

"Really? You mean, I can drop chemistry and . . ."

"Hang on, hang on. Now, look, I still think that in a year or so, all this will be water under the bridge and you will be realising that art college will be a waste of your brain. Because you do have a brain, whatever they say. But—well, if you want to switch to Lee Hill and take ceramics and art and all that bunkum once your GCSEs are over—and your mother seems to think that's what you should do—well, I suppose I'll agree."

"Dad—that's wonderful!"

"But on one condition. You still study hard at the academic stuff for these exams and you try to keep an open mind."

"Yes, Dad," said Jon dutifully. "And—thanks, Dad. I know you are disappointed in me."

His father coughed again. "No, no—I'm not. In fact, when I saw that drawing you did, I was pretty proud. I wonder where you get it from? I never could draw. Wonder what the chaps at the club would say if my son became cartoonist for the *Daily Telegraph?*" he mused.

LEE HILL SCHOOL
WESTON WAY
LEEHAMPTON

Parents' Evening—Years Nine and Ten

All parents are reminded of the parents' evening to be held on Friday, July 7th at 7 p.m. This evening is for parents and guardians and pupils. Brothers and sisters are not permitted to attend.

Tea and light refreshments will be available, proceeds to the Tennis Court Resurfacing Fund.

Signed,

Rachel Hopkirk

Rachel Hopkirk
Head of Studies

36
Designs on Dress

Ginny was not really in the mood for a Parents' Evening. She hadn't heard a word from Warwick since he left for Indonesia and she was worried about him. He might phone this evening and then she would miss him. And to make matters worse, Chelsea was hovering round her while she changed.

"Mum—if you wear that, I stay at home," declared Chelsea.

Ginny sighed. "Mum, did you hear what I said?" Chelsea repeated.

"Oh, Chelsea, what is the matter with you?" said her mother. "What is wrong with this suit?"

"Mothers don't wear shorts suits. Not normal mothers anyway. Not mothers with knobbly veins at the backs of their knees."

"Oh my God, where?"

"Only a little one," appeased Chelsea. "But please,

Mum. Take those shorts off and put a skirt on. Please. For me."

Ginny was not the only mother to be subjected to the scrutiny of her offspring. Jemma had made her mother remove her navy cord skirt and put on her best cream suit, and Laura was lecturing her mother on topics she had to avoid.

"Don't talk about anything embarrassing, will you?" she said. "Don't go on about Melvyn and you, or about Dad and the Bestial B, or the house . . . "

"Laura, I am going to school to discuss YOU. Your ability or otherwise in maths, French, history—not to hold forth about our private business. Remember, it's not me who washes our dirty linen in public."

"Oh that's right, rake up the past, throw my mistakes in my face, why don't you? Just say the bare minimum, okay?" demanded Laura.

"Mum," said Sumitha, "Dad won't make a scene at Parents' Evening, will he?"

"Why should he?" asked her mother.

"Well, he's still cross about my hair, isn't he? If he says anything at school . . . "

"Of course he won't—after all, it wasn't the teachers who cut your hair, was it?"

"No—but I don't want him to go on about discipline and English kids and . . . "

"Sumitha," said her mother, "your father will be fine. Trust me."

"Thanks, Mum."

Mrs. Banerji wished she felt as confident as she sounded.

37 Mums–2 Teachers–0

In the event, the four girls returned home from the parents' evening in varying degrees of shock and amazement.

Laura's mother had taken on the might of Miss Hopkirk, who had been endeavouring to teach English to Years Eight through Twelve since the Middle Ages and looked like an undernourished weasel.

She had declared that Laura's work had dropped off in recent months, but that of course she wouldn't blame Laura. "After all," she said coyly, "she is merely a victim. Such difficulties for a young person to handle."

Mrs. Turnbull, who was premenstrual and whose waistband was digging into her flesh, reminding her at three-minute intervals that the Hip and Thigh Diet called, said, "And what difficulties are those, Miss Hopkirk?"

Miss Hopkirk threw a sidelong glance at Laura. "Well, the—er, the—at this age—er—one doesn't like to dwell, but er—the domestic upheavals are obviously taking their toll. One parent, you know..."

At this point, Ruth's hormones staged a walk-out. "Are you implying, Miss Hopkirk, that my daughter's falling marks are my fault? That I am wholly to blame for a decline in grammatical standards? Do I write her confounded essays? Am I responsible for late prep? Perhaps, Miss Hopkirk, I am also the cause of global warming, rising prices..."

"Mum!" hissed Laura.

"Oh, Mrs. Turnbull." Miss Hopkirk's neck elongated itself in fury and turned a livid shade of violet. "I only meant that since Laura has lost a parent, she..."

"No, *you* listen, Miss Hopkirk. Laura has not lost a parent. She has not even temporarily mislaid one. Her father is alive and well and sees her regularly."

"Oh yes, but . . . "

"But nothing!" snapped Mrs. Turnbull. "Laura is a great kid. Most of the time she does her best. She is loved by me, by her father, by her whole family. If

her work has dropped off, could it possibly be because she finds your teaching uninspiring? Or because she is a normal teenager who spends three hours on the telephone and ten minutes doing homework? Whatever the cause, we will sort it out. Laura and me. And her father. Without nasty insinuations from dried up old spinsters like yourself. Good evening!"

Laura was lost for words.

Miss Hopkirk had a hot flush, two Anadin, and a cup of tea and settled down to see that nice Mrs. Gee from the newspaper. At least there was a mother who knew what was what.

"It is surprising, Mrs. Gee, that with a mother as talented as yourself, Chelsea produces some very mediocre English literature critiques," she simpered.

"Miss Hopkirk, my daughter is a person. She is not a carbon copy of me, nor would she want to be. Chelsea is brilliant at science, she doesn't faint at the sight of blood as her mother does, she can add up and get the right answer first time, and she is going to be a vet. I do not believe, Miss Hopkirk, that when splinting the leg of an Alsatian, one needs the ability to analyse Dickens's use of the past participle. Good evening!"

Miss Hopkirk had another cup of tea and a sniff of lavender oil to calm her nerves. Modern parents had no idea.

"Jemma's grasp of languages is excellent," said Mr. Horage, flicking through a folder of French and German essays and wondering why Mrs. Farrant was wearing what appeared to be a wedding suit to Parents' Evening. "Really excellent."

Jemma grinned. Mrs. Farrant looked suitably impressed.

"And, of course, Jemma will benefit enormously from the forthcoming trip to Paris," he said.

Jemma gulped. Mrs. Farrant said "Paris?" in tones of one trying to translate Arabic.

"I hadn't actually told Mum yet," said Jemma.

"Told me?" said Claire.

Jemma produced a grubby note from her blazer pocket.

SCHOOL TRIP TO
LES MOULINS CENTRE, PARIS

Dear Parent,

During the first week of the school summer holidays, Mr. Horage, Miss McConnell, and Mrs. Sandell will be taking a party of Year Nine and Ten students to Paris.

Accommodation will be in dormitories at Les Moulins Centre, within easy reach of the main sights and in addition to taking part in language activities, students will have the opportunity of sightseeing, shopping and spending time with French families in their own homes.

The cost of the trip will be £227 and a deposit of £30 is required in order to secure a place.

Yours sincerely,

Jeremiah Horage

Jeremiah Horage
Head of French

"Oh, I don't know, I really don't," murmured Claire. "They're very young to . . . "

"Mum, pleeeeese!"

"I'm sure you and Jemma need to talk it through," said Mr. Horage tactfully. "But do let me assure you that with Jemma's linguistic talents, it would be so good for her to put them to use in their place of origin, so to speak." He tittered a teacher's titter.

"I think I will be the judge of what is good for Jemma, Mr. Horage," said Claire.

"Mum, " hissed Jemma.

Sumitha sat sandwiched between her mother and father. Since the hair cut incident last week, her father had hardly spoken to her.

Now she was praying hard that the teachers would have something nice to say about her.

"And how is Sumitha progressing?" asked Rajiv.

"Very well," said Mr. Ellwood. "She's a generally good all-rounder—with, of course, a special talent for drama, dance, and singing—but you know that." Rajiv nodded.

"She tells me she wants to go into broadcasting," said Mr. Ellwood. "She'll make you very proud one day, fronting *This Morning!*" He laughed.

"She has been showing off since birth," chuckled

    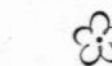

Chitrita. Sumitha squirmed.

"You'll be auditioning for the school production next term, of course?" Mr. Ellwood asked Sumitha. She nodded eagerly.

"Production?" enquired Rajiv.

"*Oliver!*" said Mr. Ellwood. "We're hoping that Sumitha might make a very suitable Artful Dodger—and now the haircut is just the ticket too!"

Rajiv sniffed.

"But what of her behaviour?" he enquired. "How does she conduct herself?"

Mr. Ellwood looked surprised. "Behaviour?" he asked. "Sumitha is charming, helpful, and very determined," he smiled, glancing at her. "She knows where she is going in life, and believe me, she will get there. No one is ever going to ride roughshod over Sumitha Banerji, and in the world today that is a big plus point."

"I suppose," said Rajiv Banerji thoughtfully, "that it is."

38
Progress Is Made

"Mum, how could you? You made me look a real wimp in there—'Oh, but she's so young…!' How could you do it to me?"

"Oh, Jemma, don't go on—you don't understand. You read such dreadful things about students alone in foreign places . . . "

"MUM! It's Paris, not Cambodia. There'll be hordes of us and everything's organised. I'm hardly like to be mugged or otherwise interfered with on a trip to Printemps, am I? Please . . . "

"Well, perhaps, but even so . . . "

"Well, ask Dad, he'll say it's okay," pleaded Jemma.

Mrs. Farrant was quite sure he would—lately he seemed to be positively itching for Jemma to grow up. And all too ready to blame his wife for holding her back. What was it he had said? "If you are not careful, you'll lose her." Of course, she didn't want that, but even so…

"Mum, please will you…?"

"I'll think about it," sighed Claire. "I promise, I'll think it over."

"Thanks, Mum," said Jemma, and began praying very hard.

"Mum, you were amazing," said Laura as they drove home.

"When?" asked her mother, as if she stood up to ageing spinsters every day of her life.

"With old Hoppy," said Laura. "And Mum, did you really mean it?"

"Mean what? That she's a stupid . . . " began her mother.

"No, that you love me and Dad loves me."

"Of course I did. You know that—how could you doubt it?" Her mother gave her an affectionate nudge.

"Does Dad love me even now he's got those pair of dimbo kids living with him?"

"Of course he does, silly—you are his own child. They will never be that—and he wouldn't want it any other way."

"And you love me, too?" persisted Laura. "Even

now there's Melvyn? Even when I'm stroppy and moan about him? Even," she added, "when I don't bother with homework because I'm feeling grouchy?"

"So you admit it?" Ruth grinned. "Laura, we would both love you if you never lifted a pencil again. Mind you that would be a bit of a waste for someone who is going to become the Greatest Living Novelist, wouldn't it?"

"I suppose it would," said Laura. "I suppose," she added, "that these traumas in my life will one day make a good blockbuster." And the thought gave her renewed hope.

Ginny Gee manoeuvred the car out of the parking space.

"You were amazing, Mum," said Chelsea. "How on earth did you dare speak to old Hoppy like that?"

"Easily," said her mother. "I am sick of people assuming that just because I write for a living, you kids have to be good at English. We had it with Geneva and Warwick, you know, and I got mad then."

"I nearly collapsed when you laid into her—she looked so amazed," said Chelsea. "It'll be all round

the staffroom tomorrow morning, you know."

"I'm sorry if I embarrassed you, love," said Ginny.

"You didn't," said Chelsea. "This time," she added.

Sumitha was sitting in the back of the car thinking about *Oliver!* when her father said, "I was very proud of you tonight."

Sumitha gulped. "Thanks, Dad," she said.

"I shall look forward to the school play," he continued. "You must get me a lot of tickets—I shall bring friends from the hospital. And by the way," he added, "you look very smart."

Sumitha was speechless. And very happy.

39
Gran-diose Plans

The following day, Jemma and her mum were waiting at the station for Jemma's gran who was coming for the weekend. She'd finally replied to Jemma's letter, promising to stop off on her way to Scotland to stay with friends. Jemma was in a hopeful frame of mind. If anyone could make Mum see sense over this French trip, then Gran could. When Jemma had told Dad about the trip, he'd murmured, "That's nice, dear," and retreated behind the Lancet.

"Does that mean I can go?" Jemma had asked.

"Sort it out with your mother, love," he had muttered, "but I don't see why not."

And Mum hadn't actually contradicted him, although she had started nibbling her thumbnail and tidying the cutlery drawer, which was a sure sign that she was agitated. Now all it needed was a final push from Gran.

"There she is!" cried Mrs. Farrant. "Oh my God, what does she look like?"

Jemma's grandmother never bothered much about clothes. She tended to hurl on whatever garments fell out of her wardrobe first. Today she was wearing a pair of pink cord trousers, a bright red sweatshirt, and a green pork-pie hat. She resembled an oversized radish.

"Darlings, how wonderful to see you both—and the precious lambs!" She gestured toward Sam and the twins, who were in the back fighting with fixed concentration over a half-chewed Twix.

"Cooo-eeee!" she called suddenly, waving her arms frantically across the carpark.

"Mother! What are you doing?" muttered Mrs. Farrant.

"Good luck, Geoffrey!" she shrieked. "Sorry, dear—met this darling man on the train. He's off to an interview at Freshfoods—just wishing him luck." She waved again. "Sock it to 'em!" she shouted across the carpark.

"Mother, for heaven's sake, people are looking!" said Mrs. Farrant.

• • •

That had been the best evening ever, thought Jemma. They'd left the boys with a baby-sitter, the video of *Snow White*, and half a shopful of crisps, and she and Mum and Dad and Gran had all gone to The Dragon Palace and had fried seaweed and crispy duck and spring rolls and lychees.

It was over the jasmine tea that Jemma, with ever an eye to the main chance, ventured, "There's going to be a school trip to Paris, Gran."

"PARIS!" cried her Gran. "Gay Paree! I love Paris—when do you go, darling?"

"Well, Mum isn't totally sure that she wants me to," said Jemma.

"Why on earth not, Claire?" exclaimed Jemma's gran. "Marvellous place—all that glamour and glitz and then the food—and those museums—and the Champs-Elysées . . . "

"Well, the point is . . . " began Claire.

"Darling, how tactless of me—of course, the cash. Silly me. Now look, Jemma darling, I shall pay for the trip—it shall be your birthday and Christmas present combined. Of course Mum was worried about you going, she's got the twins starting school any minute, and all those shoes and uni-

forms and things. And your father is NHS—I keep telling him private is where the money is, but he's socially aware, aren't you, Andrew dear? But worry not, I shall pay. Oh, and darling, you must try the frogs' legs in garlic butter—oh, and those dear little *pains chocolats* you get for breakfast."

"But Mother, it wasn't the money, it was . . ." began Claire, nudging her husband who made no move to enter the conversation.

"Don't thank me—I love to do it. Now, who's for more tea?"

40 The End of All My Hopes and the End of All My Dreams . . .

Laura was over the moon. Her dad had just phoned to say that the Bestial Betsy was taking her snotty kids to visit her mother in Eastbourne and would Laura like to spend the weekend with him?

"Oh brilliant, Dad," Laura enthused.

"I'll pick you up at ten o'clock," he said. "We'll go for lunch at The Coach and Horses if you like. I've something exciting to tell you."

Laura's heart leapt. Perhaps he was coming home.

"Is Mum there?" he asked.

This was it, thought Laura. He is coming home.

"No, she's gone for an interview for a job—school secretary somewhere or other," said Laura, the disapproval showing in her voice.

"Well, good for her—tell her I asked after her. And that I've got something for her. See you Saturday then."

Laura hung up and gave herself a hug. Two days with Dad and no BB. And Dad had asked after Mum—so he must still love her. And he'd got something for her.

Laura heard her mum's car pull into the drive. Well, judder into the drive actually, its rapidly dying parts groaning and creaking. Mum said she was putting off having it serviced till her ship came in. Apparently it hadn't left port yet.

"Hi, Mum," said Laura. "How did you get on? Would you like a cup of coffee?" Laura's good news was making her feel charitably disposed to the world.

Laura's mother looked fed up. "A coffee would be bliss," she said, slumping into a chair. "I didn't get the job."

"Bad luck," said Laura sympathetically. "What went wrong?"

"Oh, the usual—'Well, Mrs. Turnbull, you haven't worked for twelve years and your keyboard skills are rather weak and . . . ' on and on." She

sighed. "I thought that a primary school would be just right, but it seems they are all computerised now. I'll just have to take a course, I suppose."

"Dad phoned." Laura waited for her mother's joyous response.

"Oh yeah."

"He sent his love." Laura felt it politic to adapt her father's actual words in order to give them more impact.

"Well, it's a pity he didn't send a cheque instead, that would have been a sight more use to me." Laura's mum looked suspiciously near to tears.

"He's invited me for the weekend," said Laura, not really knowing what to do. "He said he'll take me to The Coach and Horses for lunch. We haven't been there for ages."

"Oh, that's right, ram it down my throat that I can't afford to take you out to lunch," said Laura's mum. "Well, I hope you have fun, but then of course you will. You'll be getting away from me, won't you?"

"Mum, I didn't mean that, I just meant . . . "

But her mother had rushed upstairs.

"Dad's here!" Laura called to her mother on Saturday morning.

Ruth came downstairs and said, "Hi, Peter," and looked uncomfortable.

"Hi there," he said. "Er, by the way, I've got this for you."

This is it, thought Laura. It'll be a romantic card or a pressie. She decided to make herself scarce so that the great reunion could take place in private.

Ten minutes later, she went downstairs. Her mum was sitting on the settee chatting happily. Her dad was laughing. It's going to be okay, said Laura. He'll be coming home any day.

"Right, are you set?" asked her dad.

They want it to be a surprise, thought Laura. I won't say a word.

"Yes, Dad," she said. She thought her mum might be coming too, seeing as how they were getting on so well, and was a bit surprised when she stayed put. Still, thought Laura, I expect Dad will want to tell me the news on his own. And she prepared to be amazed.

"That was great, Dad." Laura had just polished off a dish of garlic mushrooms, scampi and chips, and a double fudge chocolate nut sundae.

"Good, glad to see your appetite is still intact.

And now, I've a surprise for you."

Here it comes, thought Laura.

"We're going on holiday and we want you to come too," said her father, spooning the sugar into his coffee.

Wonderful, thought Laura. A family holiday again. Just the three of them. Everything was going to be all right.

"Oh, Dad, that's terrific," said Laura, and for one minute she thought she was going to cry.

"Only we decided to make it somewhere a bit special," said her dad. "I know you love Cornwall, but we wanted somewhere further afield. So we thought we'd go to Brittany."

"Brittany?" gasped Laura. "As in France?"

Her father laughed. "Well, last time I checked it was in France, yes," he said.

"Oh mega brill," cried Laura.

"I take it that is a yes, is it?" queried her father.

"Oh yes, yes yes," said Laura.

"I'm glad," he said, taking her hand across the table. "And Betsy will be too. She has been so anxious to get to know you better."

Laura felt sick.

"Betsy?" she said, her voice a mere whisper.

"Yes, she's been complaining that she doesn't see enough of you to get to know you," he added. "Two whole weeks will give you both plenty of time."

"But I thought—you mean, you want me to come on holiday with you and—her?"

"Of course—I wouldn't go and leave her behind now, would I?" Her father laughed nervously.

Suddenly it was all too much. All the hoping and believing that everything was going to be all right and now this. Laura jumped up from the table.

"Well, you jolly well should," she shouted. "You should come with me and Mum because we're your family, not that big-nosed cow and her horrid dimbo kids." She started to cry. "Mum said you loved me but you don't love me because if you did, you would come home where you belong. I HATE YOU!" And she ran out of the restaurant.

Her father stood up slowly and tried to ignore the sixteen pairs of eyes fixed on him from various corners of the dining room. He had never felt so embarrassed in all his life.

"I think I had better come in," said Peter ruefully when he landed on Ruth's doorstep with a tear-stained Laura and chronic indigestion.

Half an hour later, after her father had assured her that love doesn't come in rations and that just because you love one person doesn't mean you can't love another; and her mother had repeated dozens of times that she wanted Laura and her dad to be friends and that just because they couldn't manage to live together anymore did not mean they were deadly enemies; and Peter had said he was sorry that Laura's mum had been on edge lately and that it was partly his fault because he had been waiting to sell the house so he could give Laura's mum more money (which he had now done); Laura decided that perhaps, just possibly, life wasn't totally black.

And that if Dad really wanted her to go to France, and if Mum didn't mind (which apparently she didn't because she was planning to spend the time with her friend Pat in Plymouth and have a ball and would be most upset if Laura didn't give her the chance), she'd give it a go. Of course, she wouldn't share with Sonia, that had to be understood. And she wouldn't get on with Betsy, no matter what Dad thought. But she'd go. After all, she added, France would make an excellent setting for a novel.

41 We're All Going on a Summer Holiday

The end of term was in sight. Jon was on a high—he was leaving Bellborough as soon as he had done his GCSEs! He had gone along to Lee Hill with his parents and they had arranged for him to take his A levels there—and Dad had even said that the place didn't seem so bad and he had told Mr. Leadsom, the head of art, to pay special attention to his son, who was undoubtedly going to be a leading light of the art world. Jon had cringed at that, but at least this time his father was being embarrassing for a good cause.

The final surprise had come last night. "We were thinking of having a change of holiday this summer," said his dad.

"We're getting a bit tired of Norfolk," said his mum.

"And we wondered about these," said his dad.

"Activity Holidays at Dellfield," said the brochure.

"You can do one activity in the morning and one in the afternoon," said his mum. "I'm going to do the History of architecture and learning Upholstery!" She looked more animated than she had in months.

"Thought I'd give the Golf Improvers a go and perhaps the Clay Pigeon Shooting," said his dad. "We thought that might suit you." He pointed to a page with a turned-down corner.

"The Art of the Cartoonist," it said. "Famous cartoonist, Blob, from the *Daily Record*, runs a five-day masterclass for . . . "

"That's amazing—thanks, Dad," said Jon. Five days doing nothing but drawing. Brilliant.

"You're welcome," said his dad. "Now, if you make a good impression with this Blob chap, I could take him for a meal at the end of the course and we could see if he couldn't . . . "

"DAD!"

"Sorry, son."

"So I shall be going to France too," said Laura on

the last day of term, as she and the others were emptying their lockers.

"I can't wait," said Jemma. "A whole week in Paris with no one telling me what to wear, what to eat, or when to go to bed."

"Except the Horrific H, of course," reminded Chelsea.

"Even he's better than Mum—he doesn't have a diploma in Advanced Neurotics," said Jemma. "Although she is improving," she added, not wanting to be disloyal to her mother.

"We're going to Estepona," said Chelsea. "That's in Spain," she added when her friends looked blank. "Mum's been asked to write about some new holiday complex and they're giving us a cheapie holiday in return."

"Lucky you," said Sumitha. "I'm being dragged off to see the relatives in Calcutta. They'll all cluck and fuss and speak Bengali at top speed and drag me off to Indian films and it will be totally mega boring."

They all sighed in sympathy. "You know Jon next door," said Jemma suddenly. "That's the one Laura fancies," she added in case anyone had forgotten.

Sumitha glowered.

"I think Sumitha still likes him too," giggled Chelsea.

Laura glowered.

"Well," continued Jemma, "he's coming here after his GCSEs."

"What?" said Laura and Sumitha in unison. "Here? To Lee Hill?"

"Yup," said Jemma. "His mum told my mum. Something about him wanting to do art and design and be an illustrator or cartoonist or something equally weird."

"That's not weird," said Laura, her heart jumping.

"That's a very lucrative profession," said Sumitha defensively.

Sumitha began wondering whether Laura might eat a poisoned frog's leg and never return. Laura went all fluttery inside and thought that maybe Sumitha's relatives would ask her to stay in Calcutta forever.

"We will all write to each other while we're away, won't we?" said Jemma.

"Oh yes," they chorused. Of course they would. After all, the problem with holidays was that you got withdrawal symptoms from the telephone.

42 The Final Scene

Chelsea's mum appeared to have taken on a new lease of life ever since she heard about their cheapie holiday to Spain.

"But you'll be writing all day and trying out watersports and things," Barry had complained. "I shan't see anything of you."

"Still," he said, brightening a little, "perhaps you could wangle it so that I could get into the hotel kitchens and learn some Spanish recipes."

"Maybe," said Ginny. Or then again, maybe not.

Ginny's good mood was not due solely to the thought of two weeks in the sun. She had just been voted Regional Feature Writer of the Year, Warwick had finally phoned from some weird-sounding place in Java and assured her that he was alive, germ-free, and very happy, and Geneva had graduated with an upper second.

"I think I shall give a party," she announced one

night over what Barry assured her was Thai chicken curry. "And you mustn't cook anything this hot."

"So I thought we'd have a party before the summer holidays," she told Laura's mother over the phone. "Things are looking up—Barry's been shortlisted for a job and I'm even getting on with Chelsea, which is probably the most miraculous thing of all. Can you come?"

"Love to," said Mrs. Turnbull. "Actually, things are getting better here, too. Laura is talking to me and to Peter and to Betsy, all at the same time. And she told me last night that I wasn't bad as mothers go!"

Ginny invited the Banerjis (partly because she wanted to see if Rajiv ever unwound) and the Farrants and the Josephs and a few people from work. Chelsea and her friends were going to the new Ten Up multiscreen cinema and coming home in a taxi. For the first time in ages, Ginny thought, she could let her hair down and have a good time.

At ten thirty Laura, Sumitha, Chelsea, and Jemma arrived back at Chelsea's house, where they were spending the night.

"Come on," said Chelsea. "We'll tell them we're back then we can go upstairs and put some music on."

In the doorway to the sitting-room, they stopped openmouthed in horror. There was Chelsea's dad, his hair plastered with gel, holding an upturned wine bottle like a microphone, doing an Elvis impression, with loads of wobbly pink flesh sticking out over the top of his jeans. Laura's mum was sitting on the geek's lap feeding him nacho chips and grinning stupidly. Mrs. Banerji appeared to be teaching Ginny and Mrs. Joseph and Jemma's mum to do Indian dancing while Rajiv used an upturned waste-bin to beat time. They kept collapsing in giggles because they couldn't get their fingers to bend back like you're supposed to.

"Mum! You're dancing!" accused Chelsea.

"Mum—your knickers are showing!" shouted Laura.

"Mum—what on earth are you doing?" said Sumitha.

Jemma just gulped. Her normally frumpy mother was gyrating to the music like a soul possessed.

They all looked up, mildly surprised to see their offspring home at the appointed hour.

"Oh kids," greeted Ginny, "you're back, that's nice."

"Are you lonesome to-ooo-nite?" crooned Mr. Gee to the wine bottle.

"Mum! Dad!" they all chorused, horrified at the scene of debauchery before them. "What on earth is going on?"

"We're having a little party," grinned Ginny. "A celebration."

"Do you miss me to-ooo-nite?" crooned her husband.

"Oh for heaven's sake," shouted Chelsea, "I bring my friends home and this is what we get. Come on, you lot, let's get out of here. It's pathetic!"

"Mum, how could you?" accused Laura, her forehead puckered in a frown.

"Oh come on, now, girls," said Ginny. "What is it you're always saying?"

"Oh yes, that's right." She giggled, "Please,

'Just don't make a scene!'"

Don't Be Naff!

A levels: high school diploma

Agony Aunt: advice columnist

Boot of the car: trunk

Bunches: pony tails

Bust up: fight

Bov: conflict

Brill: brilliant, wonderful

Chuffed: psyched, smugly pleased

Comprehensive: public school

Crease: crack up

Crisps: potato chips

CV: curriculum vitae (school transcript)

Gassing: talking

Git: loser, jerk

Gobsmacked: shocked

Grotty: gross

Hob: stove

Home and dry: in the clear

Jabs: shots

Jumper: sweater

Kerb: curb, gutter

Kickers: sneakers

Kit: bag, gear

Knickers: panties

Larder: pantry

Loo: bathroom

Lorry: truck

Mad: crazy

Made redundant: fired, laid off

Mate: friend

Mini-shift: mini-dress

Naf: cheesy, lame

Suss Out the Words...

Pelmets and valances: window treatments

Plaits: braids

Poxy: disgusting

Prang: dent or bump on a car

Prat: fool

Queue: line

Reading the stars: reading the horoscopes

Row: fight

Ruck: fight

Rucksack: backpack

Semi: semi-detached house

Slog: work, trudge

Snog: make out

Spaggy bol: spaghetti with Bolognese sauce

Spots: zits

Stacking system: stereo system

Street cred: reputation

Suss: find, figure out

Swish: elegant, cool

Swot: dork, nerd

Swot up: study

Trot out: come up with

Wet: naîve, clueless

LOOK OUT FOR THE NEXT BOOK IN THE

SERIES:

I THINK I'LL JUST CURL UP AND DIE

Dear Jemma,

Guess what? I'm in love! He's 17, his name is Bilu, and we met at my cousin's wedding. He is amazing! He's got these gorgeous eyes and he is really cool. The best bit of all is that even Dad thinks he's wonderful! So I'm allowed to see him. This afternoon we're all going to watch the polo match and tonight he wants to take me to the cinema. (I know I said I don't like Indian films, but out with him I'd watch them in ancient Greek!)

No time to write more—I've got to decide what to wear. Tell Laura she's welcome to Jon—I prefer older boys. By the way, I'm growing my hair long again. Bilu likes long hair.

See you soon! Isn't love wonderful?

Sumitha XXX

Jemma Farrant sighed and tossed the postcard onto the bed. How would she know whether love was wonderful or not? She'd never had a boyfriend—not that she would dare bring one home to meet her mother if she did get lucky. Jemma had only recently persuaded her mother to let her choose her own clothes; if Mrs. Farrant had her way, she would still be wearing cord pinafores and smocked dresses.

She looked at herself critically in her bedroom mirror. She was feeling fat and lumpy. All those croissant and wedges of Camembert cheese had taken their toll, most of it between her boobs and her belly button. And talking of boobs, over the past few months hers appeared to have taken on a life of their own, expanding at an alarming rate. She'd have to get a better bra; her dear mother still bought those awful beginner things that looked like two eggshells on a piece of elastic and had about as much effect.

"Why can't I look like Chelsea?" she thought, yanking her hair into a tartan scrunchie. "I bet she's being chatted up by every Spaniard within the ten mile radius. And what's more, her Mum won't care two hoots. Life just isn't fair."

Get Chuffed!

The Fab 5 are back with 2 new books!

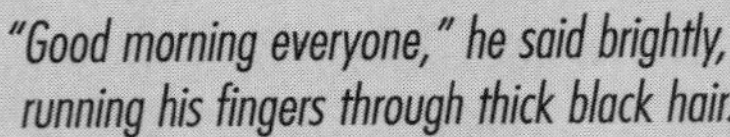

"Good morning everyone," he said brightly, running his fingers through thick black hair. "I'm Paul Sharpe and I'm your new science teacher."

Not bad, thought Laura. This is better, thought Chelsea. He is without exception the most gorgeous guy I have ever seen, thought Sumitha.

What will happen with the girls' new teacher? Brush up on your science skills in ***How Could You Do This to Me, Mum?***

You look lovely, he said silently in his head.
No, too naff.
Can't wait for later, he rehearsed.
No, too much of a come-on.
I think I'm in love with you, perhaps?
No, too slushy.
"I like prawns," he said.

Will Jon ever get a clue about girls? Read the final outcome in ***Where Do We Go From Here?***

In Bookstores September 1999

Chuffed=psyched.